SOUL
BAPTISM

SOUL BAPTISM

BY

Lucian J. Gandolfo

ARPress
45 Dan Road Suite 5
Canton MA 02021

Hotline: 1(888) 821-0229
Fax: 1(508) 545-7580

Ordering Information:

Quantity sales. Special discounts are available on quantity purchases by corporations, associations, and others. For details, contact the publisher at the address above.

Printed in the United States of America.

ISBN-13:   Paperback   979-8-89356-961-2
             eBook   979-8-89356-962-9

Library of Congress Control Number: 2024909871

CONTENTS

Endorsements

My wife and I, along with our three children, have been greatly blessed to be spiritually and morally enriched as a result of our thirty-year friendship and fellowship with Lucian Gandolfo. We discovered, in the early years of our acquaintance, that my stepmother and her entire family of ten siblings, came to be followers of Christ through the ministry of Lucian's parents while serving as missionary pastors in Bologna, Italy.

Lucian's background as a pastor's son, combined with a long and successful career as an FBI SPECIAL AGENT and an ordained minister, motivated me to invite him, on several occasions, to minister in our church in Montreal. During these ministry and family times, I discerned he was a minister of sterling character & integrity. I observed his powerful influence among young adults and the congregation as a whole. It was also during these times of preaching and teaching that I concluded Lucian was indeed a student of the Word.

As I read the book, several sermon ideas were born in my spirit. I trust the same will happen to fellow ministers. Accordingly, I wholeheartedly recommend the reading of his book 'SOUL BAPTISM'. You will definitely sense your soul being fed and your spirit enlightened as you read the book and study the biblical references that support the premise of Lucian's writings.

~ DAVID DISTAULO, General Superintendent, Canadian Assemblies of God

As a former pastor in Newark, NJ, and Brooklyn, New York, and as a former Special Agent in the FBI, Lucian Gandolfo is well qualified to deal with the tensions that separate people, both in the Church, and out. In his book, *Soul Baptism*, an attempt is made to narrow the theological division among Christians over three primary issues: the sovereignty of God, versus the free will of man; the doctrine of eternal security, versus falling from grace; and the meaning of baptism with the Holy Spirit. How well Bro. Gandolfo achieves his desired objective for a greater degree of Christian harmony and understanding will be determined by the reader. What is commendable is his effort to bring a closer unity among God's people. This is done with Scripture, and thoughtful arguments. For that, he is to be commended, and his book is highly recommended. *"Behold, how good and how pleasant it is for brethren to dwell together in unity!" (Psalm 133:1).*

~ STANFORD E. MURRELL, Th.D., Founder of Redeeming Grace Ministries

This is a Mini-Library of theological writings that cover major Pentecostal doctrines suitable for serious students of the Bible. The author covers every important truth, including: The nature of God and Man; an in-depth study of salvation; the work of the Holy Spirit in Baptism; ending up explaining the meaning of *Soul Baptism*. The reader will find this helpful in discipleship teaching, sermon building, and for any believer it is a great addition to acquiring strong Bible knowledge. Bible School students and graduates will find this filling in gaps in their Bible training. I highly recommend *Soul Baptism*.

~ DONALD WILKERSON, Co-Founder of Teen Challenge (Teen Challenge was founded in 1958, in Brooklyn, NY, with Don's late brother David Wilkerson)

Rev. Lucian Gandolfo examines the conflict faced by every believer in the battle for the mind. This book is a must for serious students of the Word of God. The understanding of the spirit-soul tension brings light on the true victory for which Christ has died and made us free.

~ PAUL JOHANSSON, President Emeritus of Elim Bible Institute and College

ACKNOWLEDGMENTS

I grew up in a Pentecostal home. My mother's parents were converted from Roman Catholicism to evangelical Christianity (Pentecostalism) when she was a little girl in Rome, Italy. My father's parents, immigrants to the United States from Sicily, were converted to evangelical Christianity (also Pentecostal) in lower Manhattan, New York City, two years prior to his birth. Although my father was born in New York City, he spent his early youth in Sicily and then Rome, Italy. He even served in the Italian Army for seven years, and during World War II. After the war he served as a representative throughout northern Europe in the capacity of an Evangelist for the Youth for Christ International ministry.

I was born in Chicago, Illinois. When I was two years old, my parents were sent by the Christian Church of North America (CCNA) as missionaries to start a new church work in Bologna, Italy. Politically, that region of northern Italy was very socialistic and atheistic, and difficult to evangelize. As I recall it, my mother said that early on they had developed a good rapport with some local Baptists who were kind and encouraged them. We spent five years in Bologna and the little church that was started in 1956 endured, and still exists today.

From the age of seven on, I grew up in New York City. All of my church experience was within the CCNA Pentecostal fellowship (later renamed the International Fellowship of Christian Assemblies, IFCA). For a number of years my father simultaneously pastored three churches: A congregation in Astoria, Queens; one in lower Manhattan;

and a storefront evangelistic outreach mission in Long Island City. But it wasn't until the age of 21 when God began to get my attention and draw me unto Himself. I surrendered my life to the Lord Jesus Christ and immediately sensed a call to ministry. My first experience of sensing the Lord's powerful touch on my life, and His strong love and acceptance, was while attending youth camp in Malaga, New Jersey, where God mightily used his servant, Robert L. Bartlett, Jr., in evangelistic youth and young adult ministry. Bob Bartlett was at that time Director of the Teen Challenge Center based in Philadelphia, PA, and would come each summer to preach at the camp during 'youth week.' Some years later, when Rev. Bartlett was the Pastor of a church and Christian school based in Laurel, Delaware, he invited me to be the guest speaker at his school's first graduation ceremony. That was my first preaching engagement.

My initial major encounter with born-again Christians who were not Pentecostal was when I enrolled in The King's College, Briarcliff Manor, NY. Most of the students at King's were either Baptist or Presbyterian. It was interesting that the President of The King's College at that time was Dr. Robert A. Cook, because coincidentally, Dr. Cook had served as Youth for Christ International's second President during the years when my father was affiliated with Youth for Christ as one of that Ministry's evangelists in northern Europe.

During the years that I completed my undergraduate work at The King's College I was employed as a Correction Officer, and then Correction Counselor, for the State of New York Department of Correctional Services. I was assigned to the Fishkill Correctional Facility in Beacon, NY. After earning a Master of Science degree in Criminal Justice from the Long Island University, in 1984 I was offered a Special Agent position with the Federal Bureau of Investigation (FBI). My first office of assignment after graduating the FBI Academy in Quantico, Virginia, was New Orleans, Louisiana. It was there that I met, and about a year later, married my first wife Lisa. Lisa was raised as a Roman Catholic, but three years prior to our meeting she had been gloriously saved in a New Orleans Assembly of God church.

My subsequent FBI assignments took me to New York City's Brooklyn-Queens office in 1986. It was during the nine years in New

York that our four children were born. In 1994 my father went to be with the Lord and for about a year I served as the Interim Pastor of the church in Astoria, Queens (NYC), that my father had pastored for 24 years. Then in 1995 I was promoted by the FBI and transferred to FBI Headquarters in Washington, DC. In 1997 I was given charge of the FBI Resident Agency located in Scranton, Pennsylvania, and in 2002 I was again promoted and sent back to the FBI's New York Office located in Manhattan, where I headed their White Collar Crime Branch. I retired from the FBI in 2005.

During the travels of my lifetime, there have been three Baptist ministers who significantly impacted my life. Though they were all Baptists, each of these men of God was very different. Their doctrinal positions were actually incompatible with each other's! They lived in different regions of the U.S., but had they all lived in the same city, their distinct theological convictions would have kept them from having meaningful fellowship with one other. I marveled at this! Though I had the privilege to enjoy a close relationship with each of these men, as a Pentecostal there seemed to be barriers prohibiting us from fully embracing one another as we ought. These are the three men:

The first was the late J. Paul Driscoll, a Southern Baptist minister, Founder and former Pastor of the Crescent City Baptist Church located in Metairie, Louisiana. As an older man, Pastor Driscoll received me like a son. Ironically, when we first met, his own son, and daughter, were both living in New York City. Also ironically, Pastor Driscoll's son, Johnny, had experienced the baptism with the Holy Spirit at the Brooklyn Tabernacle, a well-known Pentecostal church located in Brooklyn, NY, ably pastored for many years by Jim Cymbala. So, as a Pentecostal "PK" (preacher's kid) from New York City, Pastor Driscoll seemed to be intrigued and drawn to me. Away from home and my own father, I enjoyed the times of meaningful fellowship and ministry we shared together. I was impressed with his evangelistic zeal, his fatherly approach, and his tireless endurance for the pastoral ministry. I quickly grew to truly respect and admire this genuine man of God.

The second was Bud Calvert, an independent, fundamentalist, Baptist minister, Founder and Pastor emeritus of the Fairfax Baptist Temple (FBT) located in Fairfax, Virginia. Independent Fundamentalist

Baptists take their understanding of Christian doctrine very seriously and tend to resist any Biblical interpretation that doesn't line up with their traditions. Their deeply held beliefs prohibit them from close fellowship with other Christians who don't exactly mirror their teachings and practices. As such, when we first started attending FBT, Pastor Calvert and I were drawn to each other and quickly developed a rapport. Pastor Calvert seemed to have a sense of curiosity about my Pentecostal background because I didn't carry myself as how he imagined a 'charismatic' would. But, in order to join FBT it was required by their established practices that I be re-water baptized. What I always knew as 'water baptism,' these Baptists referred to it as 'believer's baptism.' Although my Christian conversion was never questioned, the second baptism was required because the Pentecostal church where I was water baptized, which happened to have been the Astoria church where my father was the Pastor, was viewed as illegitimate. A baptism performed by an 'illegitimate' church renders the baptism invalid. Hence the necessity for a re-baptism. Needless to say, a second water baptism was an unacceptable requirement for me. I was willing to either continue attending the church as a non-member, or if the Pastor preferred, seek another church. Pastor Calvert refused to accept either option. Trying to convince each other of our views seemed a stimulating challenge for each of us. To his credit, Pastor Calvert conducted a Biblical study of the Corinthian church and concluded that if Paul referred to the 'charismatic' Corinthians as "*saints*" (**1 Corinthians 1:2**) then perhaps a second baptism wasn't required for me after all! I was very impressed with Pastor Calvert's character and discipline, as well as with his willingness to modify a long-established local church policy that when contrasted to God's truth was recognized as having some room for adjustment. My two oldest children were later water baptized at FBT by Pastor Calvert. Bud Calvert was also very instrumental in driving me into deeper study so to better understand Christianity and my own Pentecostal beliefs. Had I not been challenged so strenuously by Pastor Calvert's deep convictions I may never have been able to write this book.

The third Baptist minister that significantly impacted my life was the late Marvin Rosenthal, Founder of Zion's Hope, and of the former Holy Land Experience based in Orlando, Florida. Before ever even meeting Brother Rosenthal, I had read some of his writings and listened to his teaching tapes while on long business-related drives. I absorbed his sound teaching like a sponge. On more than a few occasions I nearly swerved off of my driving lane while trying to scribble on a scratch pad, notes of insightful nuggets of truth that I didn't want to forget. Rosenthal opened up to me so much of what I didn't know about Judaism, and what I had previously missed in the Gospels, the epistles, and in the prophetic passages of Scripture. In my subsequent role as both a District and national CCNA/IFCA Presbyter, some years ago Rosenthal accepted my invitation to come to New York City to speak at a regional Pentecostal ministers' conference that I was organizing. Though he was initially reluctant, perhaps fearing rejection, and though I was questioned by some of my fellow Pentecostal ministers and overseers about my choice of guest speaker, Marvin Rosenthal was a true blessing to us all. I was impressed by his sensitivity, respect and graciousness. I credit Rosenthal with deepening the effectiveness of my own preaching and teaching, and with instilling within me the desire to finish my doctoral studies in theology.

I thank God for allowing me to cross paths with these His servants. All of the ones mentioned thus far, including my father Michael Gandolfo, Bob Bartlett, Paul Driscoll, Bud Calvert, and Marvin Rosenthal, were used of God to enrich my life. But there have been others, many within the CCNA/IFCA fellowship, as well as those from without, like Assembly of God Pastor Ernest Drost of Peckville, PA, and Rev. David DiStaulo of Montreal, currently the General Superintendent of the Canadian Assemblies of God, who both honored me by giving me numerous opportunities to minister to the congregations entrusted to their care. I can't fail to mention the obscure Peter DePasquale of Arena Partners. I met him briefly, and only once in 2005, at a law enforcement event held at the Rainbow Room in New York City. Our conversation somehow included my work on "Soul Baptism." It was Peter DePasquale who hadn't even seen a transcript, that after a brief discussion about it was adamant my work was worthy of copyrighting, finishing and publishing. If it wasn't for his timely little nudge of encouragement, I may have not followed through with publishing *Soul Baptism*.

My studies that led to the original 2006 publishing of *Soul Baptism* prepared me to be a more effective minister and preacher-teacher of the Word, especially during the nearly six years as Senior Pastor of the Trinity Tabernacle of Gravesend in Brooklyn, New York. More recently, in 2020, Dr. Stanford E. Murrell, a gifted Reformed Christian, felt moved to create a Study Guide as an accompaniment to the original *Soul Baptism*. What an encouragement he was! This servant of God from the improbable Reformed wing of Christianity believed in my work enough to voluntarily undertake that project. His unexpected support propelled me to re-publish a partially revised edition of Soul Baptism in 2022. The revisions did not alter the original message content, but attempted to add some expanded clarification for my tendency to an 'intense' writing style. This third 2024 revision endeavors to add some additionally needed clarifications and more supporting Scriptures.

Prior to ordination in 1996, I was honored to serve in CCNA/IFCA District and National youth ministry offices, as well as in assistant and interim pastorships in New York. Then after ordination, I served as both a District and National CCNA/IFCA Presbyter, an Associate Pastor, and twice as a Senior Pastor, in Newark, NJ, and in Brooklyn, NY. The Trinity Tabernacle of Gravesend, the Brooklyn church, where I served as its Senior Pastor from mid-2007 to early 2013, was originally an historical landmark Reformed church!

In early 2022 I was elected to serve as a Deacon, at the Beacon Baptist Church, an Independent Fundamental Baptist church located in Melbourne, FL, with my wife Denise active in their women's ministry. By the end of 2022 I was elevated to Head Deacon. Beacon Baptist Church's former Senior Pastor, Wayne Guinn, who was promoted to glory in July 2023, not only initially encouraged me to accept the Deacon's office, but had given me numerous opportunities to teach and minister to the assembly under his stewardship. Being fully aware of our differing understandings in the doctrinal areas of spiritual gifts and eschatology, I so appreciated his trust and confidence! Amazingly, by September 2023, I was elected to replace Pastor Guinn as the Senior Pastor of Beacon Baptist Church! I am so amused by how God saw fit to once again place me and my wife in unlikely places of service to His glory! To all the above-mentioned great men used of God in my life, I give my heartfelt acknowledgment.

I have found there is much Reformed Christians and Evangelicals (i.e., Baptists and Pentecostals), can admire and learn from one another. The theological intellect of the Reformed, the faith-disciplines of the Baptists, and the Spirit-anointed ministries of Pentecostals, are not antithetic to one another! Rather, all of these qualities ought to be sought after and embraced by all! I have benefitted from my Christian friends and mentors, and I write this book to share what I have learned from them, and in conjunction with that, what I've discovered from God's Word.

For the sake of an initial clarification to better understand the message of *Soul Baptism*, which is written to unite divergent Christian denominations, here's a very brief synopsis of what I've observed about the "Big Three" schisms of Protestant Christianity:

1. "Sovereignty vs. Free Will" – Reformed Christianity emphasizes 'sovereignty' in God's salvation program, thereby fully embracing the Calvinistic doctrines of mankind's 'total depravity,' 'predestination,' 'limited atonement,' 'irresistible grace,' and 'eternal security.' Whereas, the 'free-will' of man in the process of receiving salvation is generally insisted upon by most Baptists, Pentecostals, as well as Methodists and other denominations stemming from the holiness movements of the 19th Century. While there are 'Calvinistic Baptists,' the "Free-Will Baptists" adopted their name to more loudly emphasize their rejection of "5-Point Calvinism."

2. "Eternal Security vs. Falling From Grace" – Reformed Christianity, most Baptists, and relatively few Pentecostals, embrace the doctrine of 'eternal security,' which states once genuinely saved, a believer cannot lose or forfeit his/her salvation. Many Pentecostals adhere to an Arminian doctrine that emphasizes a strive for holiness as a condition for evidencing and keeping one's salvation, and for the avoidance of 'falling from grace.' Traditional Baptists also teach holiness, but believe a failure to achieve a desired Biblical standard of holy living does not threaten a true believer's salvation. Reformed believers believe God's sovereignty will persevere His elect.

3. "Cessationism vs. Continuationism" – Reformed Christians and Baptists generally agree that the 'manifestation' gifts of the Holy Spirit; i.e., tongues and interpretation, prophecy, healing, miracles, words of knowledge and wisdom, supernaturally infused faith and discerning of spirits, ceased to operate in the New Testament Church once the inspired canon of New Testament Scriptures (Matthew through Revelation) was completed. Baptists call these "sign-gifts," but Pentecostals and Charismatics disagree with the Baptists. They insist these gifts of the Holy Spirit were intended by God to operate for the totality of the Church Age, and not for the First Century only.

Finally, I want to thank my wife, Denise, for all of her support and belief in me at a time in life when I was resolved that perhaps I had already concluded all of the Kingdom contributions of my lifetime. Denise has been insistent that God wasn't finished with me yet, and prayerfully continued to encourage me not to neglect using the gifts God entrusted to me. So, with her strong support, and the encouragement of others, I submit this third 2024 revised edition of 'Soul Baptism.'

"SOUL BAPTISM" OUTLINE of Discussion Points

ACKNOWLEDGEMENTS

- Author's Pentecostal upbringing and exposure to non-Pentecostal believers
- Author's adult secular & ministerial career, and his influencers
- Introduction to the "Big Three" doctrinal schisms of Protestant Christianity

INTRODUCTION

❖ *Why divisions? - The foundational basics of Christianity*

A. Focus, Hypothesis & Goal

- Goal: Key to understanding is a 3-dimensional perspective for unity of faith
- Focus: 3-dimensional works of Triune God
- Hypothesis: "Divine Triangulation," God's foolproof 3-dimensional strategy

B. Presupposing Man's Trichotomy

- Dichotomy
- Trichotomous
- A possible solution for the two, and the trichotomous presupposition

C. Realm of the Soul - and its vulnerability

- Intellect
- Emotions
- Will
  - Exhortation to study (*not just read*) this book, and the supporting scriptures

SECTION ONE : GOD, MAN and the SPIRITUAL BATTLEFIELD

CHAPTER 1: THE TRIUNE NATURE OF GOD

❖ *Divine Triangulation*

A. The Trinity

- One triune God: Father, Son, and Holy Spirit

B. Creation of the Heavens

- The 3 heavens: Earth's atmosphere, the universe, the heavenly dimension

C. Creation of Matter

- Triangulation: As seen in creation, nature, scientific laws, preayer, works and miracles

CHAPTER 2: THE TRICHOTOMY OF MAN

❖ *Created in God's image for relationship with Him*

A. Spirit, Soul, and Body: 3 Christian Baptisms
- Regenerational baptism by the Spirit: *For re-birth of man's spirit*
- Believers' water baptism: *For man's external 'body' as a witness*
- Empowering baptism with the Spirit: *For fortification of man's soul*

B. God's Communication with Man
- God communicates through man's *spirit*

C. Satan's Communication with Man
- Satan communicates through man's *soul*
- 'Name' selections and practices that reflect our cultural mindset

CHAPTER 3: THE THREE SPHERES OF SPIRITUAL WARFARE

❖ *Satan, the world, and the flesh, as seen in Jesus' parable of the 'Sower & Seeds'*

A. Satan – *the 1st sphere*
- Seeks to counterfeit and redirect worship belonging to God, to himself
- Biblical examples of Satan's subtle deceptions

B. The World System – *the 2nd sphere*
- Ruled and influenced by Satan
- The Church is called out the world

C. The Flesh – *the 3rd sphere*
- *Weak link of man's trichotomy*
- Fleshly appetites grow, but are abated through the strengthening of the spirit

SECTION TWO: GOD, MAN, AND PERSONAL SALVATION

CHAPTER 4: THE TRINITY AT WORK IN MAN'S SALVATION

❖ *3 Persons of Godhead engaged in accomplishment of man's salvation*

A. Design of the Father – *The Architect*
- Every good gift comes down to us from the Father

B. Provided through the Son – Our *Substitution*
- By Jesus' substitutionary death, and resurrection

C. Effected by the Spirit – The *Applier* of God's gifts
- The regenerational new-birth

CHAPTER 5: THE TRICHOTOMY OF MAN AND SALVATION

❖ *3 Phases of man's completed salvation*

A. **Regeneration of man's spirit**
   - Can regeneration be reversed?
   - Calvinism vs Arminianism: strengths & weaknesses
   - The provision & exercise of *Faith*, and the examination of *Backsliding*

B. **Sanctification of man's soul**
   - Only the soul can backslide
   - Wisdom is the proper application of knowledge

C. **Glorification of man's body**
   - Futuristic
   - The end-result of man's transformational process

CHAPTER 6: THE THREE-FOLD ASPECT OF SALVATION

❖ *"Quickened," "Raised," and "Seated"*

A. **Positional**
   - Man's spirit is quickened

B. **Progressive**
   - Strengthened by discipline and Spirit's giftings

C. **Permanent**
   - Final phase of man's blessed hope

SECTION THREE: GOD, MAN, AND PROVISION FOR EMPOWERMENT

CHAPTER 7: THE THREE OFFICES OF CHRIST

❖ *The 3 primary names of God: Jehovah, Elohim, and Adonai*

A. **Christ the *Incomparable Prophet* – alludes to *Jehovah***
   - Brought God's Word to man (positional)

B. **Christ the *Ultimate* Priest – alludes to *Elohim***
   - Our Intercessor (progressive)

C. **Christ the *Glorious* King – alludes to *Adonai***
   - Returning King (futuristic)

CHAPTER 8: THE THREE FOLD WORK OF THE HOLY SPIRIT

❖ *Uniquesness of the Church Era*

A. Of Sin
- So we may believe (*positional salvation in past tense*)
- The root deception of sin us unbelief

B. Of Righteousness
- So we may be comforted (*progressive salvation in present tense*)
- The Holy Spirit is our Comforter

C. Of Judgment
- So we may be vindicated (permanent salvation in futuristic sense)
- The 'Prince of the world' is judged

CHAPTER 9: THE BAPTISM WITH THE HOLY SPIRIT

❖ *For salvation or empowerment? – 'Subsequence' & the first Acts 2 Baptism*

A. Biblical definition of the Baptism with the Holy Spirit
- The Baptizer – *Jesus Christ*
- The Apostles – *Subsequence*
- The Evidence – *Tongues*
  - Cessation of tongues?

B. Qualifications for the Baptism with the Holy Spirit
- Correctly understanding distinction helps answer Calvin-Arminian difficulties
  - Is this baptism for the unbeliever unto salvation?
  - Is this baptism for the empowerment of the believer?
  - Was Pentecost the 'birthday' of the Church?

C. The Trinity's Work in Spiritual Giftings
- Godhead engaged in three-dimensional giftings:
  - The Godhead Source – *by the same God, Lord, and Spirit*
  - The Godhead Attributes – *not humanly-limited*
  - The Godhead Gifts - 3 categories: *Ministry, Motivational, Manifestational*

CONCLUSION: THE "SOUL BAPTISM"

❖ *Bridging the "big three" doctrinal chasms within the Body of Christ*

- The Three Blessings of Romans
- The Three Seasons of God's communion with man
- The "*Divine Triangulation*" Key

A. **The "Big-3" Schisms of Faith**
- **Sovereignty vs. Free Will**
  - ○ The Five 'Solas'
  - ○ The Five Tenets of Calvinism
  - ○ T.U.L.I.P.
- **Eternal Security vs. Falling from Grace**
  - ○ Salvation is eternal
  - ○ Anointing can wane
  - ○ Rewards can be forfeited
- **Cessationism vs Continuationism**
- The 4-fold mission of the New Testament Church
- The three Christian baptisms
- The three categories of spiritual gifts
- The permanency of the 5-Fold ministry gifts

B. **The Soul Solution of Faith**
- **The Battlefield of the Soul**
  - ○ o Soul, not spirit, is where backsliding can occur
- **The Comforter of the Soul**
  - ○ Same Spirit that regenerates also fills, leads to truth, illuminates regarding things to come
- **The Empowerment of the Soul**
  - ○ The Spirit enhances the Christian's conventional means for engagement in spiritual warfare

C. **The Unity of Faith**
- *Soul Baptism's reconciliation of:*
  - ○ T.U.L.I.P. doctrines
  - ○ Security vs Falling
  - ○ Cessation vs Continuation of the Spirit's giftings
- **The "*Divine Triangulation*" perspective reconciles unnecessary divisions**
- **Final Exhortation and Call for Unity.**

INTRODUCTION

"Till we all come in the unity of the faith,
and of the knowledge of the Son of God, unto a perfect man, unto
the measure of the stature of the fullness of Christ."
Ephesians 4:13

We are living in exciting times! Even in this already postmodern era, evil is now manifesting itself at unprecedented levels. Besides the perilous wickedness, evil, corruption, and violence that rivals the pre-Flood state of affairs on the earth (**Genesis 6:5,11**), godless immorality, LGBTQIA+ agenda (*an acronym used to signify Gay, Lesbian, Bisexual, Transgender, Queer, Intersex, and Asexual people collectively*), obsessions of racism, lawlessness, injustice, abortion, and gender fluidity, have become the standard, and the operating principles of our society's major institutions. The Church has not remained unscathed, as seen in '*theological deconstruction.*' Yet, these are indeed exciting times of opportunity for the true Church of Jesus Christ because, "*where sin abounded, grace did much more abound*" (**Romans 5:20**)! God promises His graces of salvation and Church-giftings to accomplish His will, will operate exponentially greater than any abounding sin! But is the modern Church united and sufficiently prepared to face down and overcome Satan's end-time onslaught, to the glory of God?

Why has Satan been so successful instilling divisions into the Body of Christ? Perhaps, over the centuries, in a misguided pursuit for relevancy, the modern Church has lost some understanding of its true identity and purpose. In some cases, it has redefined and reinterpreted Scriptural truth. Several disappointing examples are being seen unfolding in the Christian denominations of our day! Major denominations are fractured and even formally splitting over principles of theology and doctrinal standards. Orthodoxy is being challenged and altered in order to support abortion, embrace the homosexual and transexual agenda in marriage and the clergy, and the promotion of the "Woke" agenda in their church practices! But in most less-extreme cases, 'faithful' churches have simply institutionalized themselves into partisan factions of preferred systems of doctrinal interpretations that are supported by select Scriptures and not the totality of God's Word.

However, the basics of Christianity have remained the same! Simply, that there are presently two kingdoms: God's and Satan's. Since the 'Fall' (*Adam's sin*), the scepter of spiritual world rulership was lost by Adam and taken possession of by Satan. Satan became the "*Prince of this world* (**John 14:30**)." God's Covenants prepared a people (*Israelites*) through whom God would bring forth a Deliverer (*Jesus Christ*) who would come to discomfit Satan (**1 John 3:8**), redeem His people, reclaim creation, and restore God's dominion of righteousness by bringing the Kingdom of Heaven to earth (**Matthew 4:17**). Satan and his followers would be forever cast out, and a new heaven, a new earth, and a new Jerusalem would be eternally established to the glory of God! (**Revelation 20:10-21:8**).

Though believers have experienced their salvation through a near-infinite variety of circumstances and experiences, we were all saved in the very same exact way! That is, by God's merciful grace, made possible by the sin-removing work on the Cross of the resurrected Christ, and through the renewal-application of the Holy Spirit received through repentance by faith (**Titus 3:4-7**)! However, doctrinal chasms founded on dubious theological definitions and faulty conclusions, have developed throughout the Church Age, separating even those Bible-believing, born-again, Christ-exalting believers, who all claim to agree on the authority of Scripture for their Christian orthodoxy and as their sole basis of faith.

Of the primary issues that separate us, perhaps three of the most contentious are; "sovereignty" versus "free-will," "eternal security" versus "falling from grace," and "cessationism" versus "continuationism."

Concerning the 'cessationism-vs-continuationism' debate, a brief review of all the spiritual giftings is mentioned in *Soul Baptism* (esp. Chapter 9, Section C-3), but for the purposes of this book, discussion regarding this third contention will mainly focus on whether the baptism with the Holy Spirit is the one-time salvation experience of spiritual regeneration, or a subsequent-to-salvation spiritual endowment of empowerment. Properly understanding the 'baptism' issue can be illuminating on all the other issues, and ultimately unifying.

A. Focus, Hypothesis & Goal of this Book

A foundational key proposed in *Soul Baptism* to help unlock our understanding and attempt the reconciliation of these divergent doctrinal positions, is the recognition that God is, and often acts, in "threes." God's very essence is triune, and all his creativity and doings seem to be accomplished in a three-fold manner.

Soul Baptism affirms the One triune God and presupposes the trichotomy of regenerated man. Men possess material bodies, and immaterial spirits and souls. At the moment of salvation, man's spirit is re-born and permanently regenerated from a dead to a living state. It is made alive by the Spirit of God to be able to have eternal relationship with God. The soul is defined as that inner and God-created human immaterial part of man, distinct from the spirit. The soul is man's intellect, emotions, and will. It is the human realm where spiritual warfare takes place. Scriptural research will show that the soul is also that part of regenerated man that requires continual cleansing and discipline, as well as empowerment provided for through spiritual gifts. The "Pentecostal" baptism with the Holy Spirit will be shown to be a divine aid for the empowerment of the soul. Hence the title of this book: "*Soul Baptism.*"

The focus of *Soul Baptism* is to discuss how a holy triune God, creates, redeems, equips, preserves, and ultimately glorifies a sinful and carnal trichotomous man. The goal is to address this topic in a manner that will help bring Christians of like-faith, but from various doctrinal camps, closer together. This is not an attempt at ecumenism, which all too often demands doctrinal compromise. But rather, the affirming of biblical truths we all hold dear, with a view to unraveling unnecessary and divisive barriers standing between genuine brethren. Seeing God's works from a three-dimensional perspective will, I believe, bridge some unnecessary doctrinal chasms.

The hypothesis of this book is that God often operates by 'triangulation.' In both the broad processes of creation and salvation, God takes three-fold approach strategies that serve to perfectly complete all his purposes, while also eliminating any possibility for error or failure. We may call this, "***divine triangulation***."

It is hoped the value of this study will be the provision of an intellectual catalyst to theological, anthropological and soteriological understanding, that will be able to potentially bridge doctrinal chasms that have existed between groups of believers for too many centuries. In my view, these gaps of disunity between philosophically opposing Christian camps are largely unnecessary. Primarily, these would be those divergent groups who in aspects of the soteriological doctrine of Eternal Security closely align themselves to either Calvinism or Arminianism. It would also be for those who would classify themselves as "Pentecostal," in contrast with others who find their Christian identity in the Reformed, Baptistic, and other "non-charismatic" mainline denominations. The intention is to help dispel some distrust between these camps with their varied doctrinal views, but who also share the same foundation of established Biblical truths, as recited in this book.

This is the hope and aim of "Soul Baptism." May God help me to lay out the intended concepts in a clear enough manner to adequately address the stated problems and suggested solutions. In these fast-moving last days, we need to advance towards the lofty goal of bridging traditionally and doctrinally separate, but Christ-blood related, Christians. We are all on the same Team!

B. Presupposing Man's Trichotomy

Throughout the Church Age Christians have argued over the question of whether man is a *dichotomy* or a *trichotomy*. In his *Lectures in Systematic Theology*, Henry Thiessen observed that, "The Western church generally held to dichotomy, while the Eastern church generally held to trichotomy."[1] That may have shifted somewhat over the centuries, but the Church still struggles with this question of the immaterial, or 'spiritual,' part of man.

1) Dichotomy

Those who hold the dichotomy view believe that man is a two-part being, with material and immaterial components. Dichotomists view the spirit and soul as interchangeable terms for the immaterial part of man. In Paul Enns' work, *The Moody Handbook of Theology*, Enns notes that from the dichotomists' point of view, "the non-material part of man is the soul and spirit, which are of the same substance; however they have a different function."[2] J. Oliver Buswell, a strong dichotomist, makes this statement in his work, *A Systematic Theology of the Christian Religion*, "There is nothing ... to show that the difference between 'soul' and 'spirit' is other than a difference of functional names for the same substantive entity, the same kind of difference that obtains between 'heart' and 'mind'."[3] Buswell ratchets up his rhetoric by declaring heretical the, "notion in the minds of most trichotomists ... that man as body, soul, and spirit is a reflection of the Trinity, Father, Son, and Holy Spirit, and that this alleged trichotomous nature of man is what constitutes the image of God, or at least an aspect of that image."[4] Furthermore, Buswell dismisses the trichotomists' **1 Thessalonians 5:23**[5] 'proof-text' for their view, and sarcastically counters, "It is surprising that church history has not developed a "quadratomy" based on the saying of Jesus, *'Thou shalt love the Lord thy God with all thy heart, and with all thy soul, and with all thy strength, and with all thy mind'* ... (**Luke 10:27**)."[6] Paul Enns notes that, "Men like Augustine and Anselm held to this (dichotomous) view."[7] Reformed theology is generally *dichotomous*.

2) Trichotomy

Trichotomists argue that man is a tri-part being, and that the spirit and soul are distinct components of man's immaterial makeup, "...both in substance and in function. The body is seen as world-conscious, the soul as self-conscious, and the spirit as God-conscious."[8]

In, *Trichotomy: A Study of the Spirit, Soul & Body*, Austin Barton puts it this way, "We are a spirit, we live with a soul, we live in a body. Physical contact with the world is made by the body. Mental contact is made with the mind. With the spirit we contact God – who is a Spirit."[9] Finally, Gleason L. Archer, in his *Encyclopedia of Bible Difficulties*, refers to the original biblical text and observes, "It is to be noted, therefore, that there is distinction between 'spirit' (*ruah*) and 'soul' (*nepes*) in the Old Testament, just as there is between *pneuma* and *psyche* in the New Testament."[10] Again, Paul Enns notes that, "Originally, the Greek and Alexandrian church Fathers held this (trichotomous) view, including men like Origen and Clement of Alexandria."[11]

3) Presupposition

In his book, *Spirit, Soul & Body*, Lester Sumrall presents an interesting view on this subject that should be mentioned. Sumrall asserts that,

"Outside of the Bible, man is a dualism or two-part creature. Psychiatry, psychology, and philosophy teach that man is two parts. They think he is inside and outside, topside and bottomside. The Word of God says that man is three."[12]

What Sumrall concludes is that Adam was originally a trichotomy. When Adam fell, his spirit "died," and he became a dichotomy. Sumrall says that as result of the fall, "Adam's nature changed from a spiritual being into a soulical being."[13] Ever since Adam, unregenerate man is born as a dichotomy until he is 'born again,' or regenerated by the Spirit of God, at which time he returns to his God-intended trichotomous state. Therefore, unregenerate man's "3-cylinder motor" operates on only "two cylinders" until such a time as he is converted back into the family of God.

Since the weight of evidence points to a distinction between man's soul and spirit (dichotomists stress the distinction is only in function), and since the trichotomous concept seems to be borne out by consistency in pattern of the many other tri-part aspects of God's works, some of which are mentioned in this study, we will presuppose the trichotomous view to be most correct and will use it as a basis for discussion in this book. Especially so, in light of Sumrall's view, because in this study we will be primarily focusing on regenerated man. Baptists and Pentecostals are generally *trichotomous*.

C. Realm of the Soul

Most commonly, man's soul is defined as his intellect, emotions, and will. Henry Thiessen describes it as the, "reason, conscience, and will."[14] Austin Barton puts it this way, "The soul – the second dimension of triune man – is the personality. It is the mind, the will, the temperaments, and the emotions. It is the middle you, the 'go-between' or intermediary between the spirit and the body."[15]

A premise of this study is that the unfortified soul is that vulnerable immaterial part of man through which Satan is able to easily communicate and tempt, so to seek the ultimate destruction of the whole man.

1) Intellect

The knowledge of God is made possible by two things; the revelation of God, and the endowments of man. The human endowments are mental and spiritual. The intellect of man refers to the ability of his mind, his thought processes, his ability to learn, discover, understand, reason, construct and invent. Raw facts are insufficient for the human mind. The human intellect requires more than just an accumulation of facts. It seeks for a systemization of knowledge. We endeavor to comprehend the relationship of facts, and to organize this knowledge so that we may draw inferences and understandable conclusions. God gifted man with intellect, not only for the ability to thrive on the earth, but with the ultimate capacity to have relationship, and even the ability to "*reason*" (**Isaiah 1:18**), with God his creator.

In support of the triangulation hypothesis, even in this subdivision on the intellect, Sumrell recognizes a three-dimensional challenge for man's intellect. He asserts that, "The three major areas of education with which all of us must grapple is (knowing) 'Who is God?,' (to) 'Know your fellowman,' (and to) 'Know yourself.'"[16] Sumrell argues that understanding this truth regarding the "total man" is the key to the, "very core and center of (resolution to) all human problems."[17] Barton adds that the soul is the avenue of the Enemy's attack, primarily through the mind, but also through our temperament or emotions.[18] I support this assessment, as it is aligned with the hypothesis of this book.

2) Emotions

Human emotions relate to sensibility, to feelings, such as love, anger, hatred, joy, sorrow, remorse or fear. Emotions are intricately embedded in the human soul and play a crucial part in man's decisions and behavior. Thiessen places emotions at the center of the soul as follows, "Intellect enables man to discern between what is right and what is wrong; sensibility appeals to him to do the one or the other, and will decides the issue."[19] Thiessen sees intellect and sensibility as the conscience, which he defines as, "the knowledge of self in relation to a known law of right and wrong."[20]

3) Will

"Free" will is man's power to choose to do or not do what he is able to do. Thiessen elaborates on this limitation by noting that,

> "Man's will is free in the sense that man can choose to do anything in keeping with his nature. Man can will to walk, but not to fly. To walk is in keeping with his nature, but to fly is not. ... This is likewise true in the moral realm. Adam could will to sin or not to sin. After the fall, man's ability to sin became man's inability not to sin. Man may now desire to change ... but he is unable by merely willing to change his moral state."[21]

This insufficiency leaves man frustrated but not without remedy. Barton notes, "An amazing truth is: God does not beat down the will. He wants you to submit your will to Him."[22] The submission of one's human will is a purposeful act of faith which removes barriers for God to accomplish His will in and through us. God's sovereignty is not infringed upon by man's free will, and man's exercise of his free will does not impinge God's sovereignty!

As can be seen by these few cited theologians' quotations, the realm of the soul is complex and cannot be over simplified. However, as previously stated, for the purposes of this study it is sufficient to embrace the simple definition of man's soul as the immaterial "intellect, emotions, and will." These three form the three human attributes of 'personality.'

As previously stated, this book *Soul Baptism* is based on the concept that God is and acts in "threes." To bring emphasis to this notion, I have placed between the three-part introduction and three-part conclusion, the body of this paper, which has been composed in three broad sections, each containing three-chapter topics. Where the chapters and topics are further subdivided, it is done so in threes.

While all inquiring persons can benefit, *Soul Baptism* is written primarily to believers who have some familiarity with basic theological concepts. The book was written not as a casual read, but with encouragement for the reader to dig deeper into the study of God's Word. You may notice it's riddled throughout with valuable 'truth nuggets,' that can spin-off deeper studies of meaningful truth! The book presents salvation from God's perspective, man's perspective, and a theological perspective. **The reader is strongly encouraged to imitate the noble Bereans (Acts 17:10-11), and to carefully review the supporting Scriptures cited throughout *Soul Baptism* that have been conveniently highlighted, and then listed in the Scripture Reference Index** at the end of the book.

On that thought, it was not by design, but perhaps not so coincidental, that this is now the third edition of *Soul Baptism*. The first edition was written in 2006. The second edition revision was published in 2022, but still lacked some important content that could have further clarified the main points being made. So hopefully, this third edition will be a bit more complete and render the important message of this book more compelling.

It should also be noted here that scholars and theologians quoted in *Soul Baptism* (*as well as those who offered endorsements for this book*), represent all three of the main doctrinal Christian camps. All Scripture quotes were taken from the Authorized King James Version of the Bible.

Introduction Endnotes

[1] Henry Clarence Thiessen, *Lectures in Systematic Theology*, (Grand Rapids: Eerdman's Publishing Co., rev. ed., 1979), 160.

[2] Paul Enns, *The Moody Handbook of Theology*, (Chicago: Moody Press, 1989), 306.

[3] J. Oliver Buswell, *A Systematic Theology of the Christian Religion*, (Grand Rapids: Zondervan, 1976), 247.

[4] Buswell, 247.

[5] *"And the very God of peace sanctify you wholly, and I pray God your whole spirit and soul and body be preserved blameless unto the coming of our Lord Jesus Christ,"* (**1 Thessalonians 5:23**).

[6] Buswell, 244.

[7] Enns, 306.

[8] Enns, 307.

[9] Austin Barton, *Trichotomy: A Study of the Spirit, Soul & Body*, (Tulsa: Harrison House, 1976), 6.

[10] Gleason L. Archer, *Encyclopedia of Bible Difficulties*, (Grand Rapids: Zondervan, 1982), 259.

[11] Enns, 306.

[12] Lester Sumrall, *Spirit, Soul and Body*, (New Kensington: Whitaker House, 1995), 11.

[13] Sumrall, 24.

[14] Thiessen, 155.

[15] Barton, 22.

[16] Sumrell, 7-9.

[17] Sumrell, 7.

[18] Barton, 23.

[19] Thiessen, 162.

[20] Thiessen, 162.

[21] Thiessen, 163.

[22] Barton, 23.

SECTION ONE:

GOD, MAN, AND THE SPIRITUAL BATTLEFIELD

CHAPTER 1
THE TRIUNE NATURE OF GOD

*"For there are three that bear record in heaven,
the Father, the Word, and the Holy Ghost: and these three are one."*
1 John 5:7

A. The Trinity

The doctrine of the Trinity is a fundamental and necessary doctrine of Christianity. Trinitarians believe there is <u>one</u> God, co-existent, co-equal, and co-eternal in three Persons (i.e., three eternal distinctions in one divine essence): Father, Son, and Holy Spirit. Each Person of the Trinity possesses all three attributes of personality (i.e., intellect, sensibility, and will). In, *GOD, I Don't Understand*, Kenneth Boa asserts that the Trinity to the human mind is an inscrutable and "superrational antinomy."[1] This in itself is a "proof" of the doctrine's truth, in that man could not have invented it, but that indeed it originates from God's special revelation of Himself to us.

Although the word "*trinity*" is not found in the Bible, the teaching of the Trinity most certainly is. Most Reformed, Baptist, and Pentecostal believers agree on this point, although there is a minority of "Oneness" or "Jesus Only" Pentecostals that deny the Trinity. The term "Trinity" was first used in the Christian Church, circa A.D. 220. In discussing use of the term "Trinity," theology Professor William E. Hordern cites the Nicene Creed as a rejection of any notion of three gods bound into some kind of unity, and credits Augustine with establishing the articulated doctrinal statement concerning the Trinity. In Hordern's, *A Layman's Guide to Protestant Theology*, he states:

> "It is clear that when we think of the Trinity, we should not try to think of three persons in our sense of the term. Augustine's interpretation became orthodox, if not universal, for the West. He believed that if man is created in the image of God, he is created in the image of the Trinity."[2]

In his book, *One God or Three?*, Stan Rosenthal, active in evangelistic Christian ministry to Jews, declares that for the purposes of outreach to Jews, the term "Trinity" is "regrettable, unfortunate, and incorrect." Rosenthal furthermore argues that, "When Christians use the term 'trinity' (which simply means 'three'), they unconsciously communicate the concept of polytheism."[3] This identification with polytheism shuts down any openness a typical Jew may have for honest discussion regarding the truth of Christianity. Rosenthal however is a steadfast Trinitarian, who prefers the term "Tri-unity" which he says better, "conveys the idea that God is one, but at the same time consists of three persons."[4]

Addressing the problem of finite man attempting to understand and describe the infinite God, Kenneth Boa insists we must do so not by relying on unaided human reasoning, but by study of the revealed Word of God. Boa states as follows:

> "Christians recognize that there are many things about God which are mysterious, incomprehensible, and superrational. God in His existence as the Three-in-One is beyond the limits of human comprehension. The Scriptures reveal not only the complete unity of the Godhead but also the equally complete distinctiveness of the three Persons who make up the Godhead. Through all eternity there is a perfect and absolute unity and diversity because the Godhead is One and Three."[5]

In dealing with the element of subordination within the Trinity, Boa states:

"In formulating a picture of the Trinity, we should also note that while the Three are equally divine and eternal, there is nevertheless a strong element of subordination. This subordination is not intrinsic (since no member is inferior to another) but relational. The Scriptures indicate an order of priority or antecedence in the way God operates and reveals Himself. The Father is especially active as the Originator, Creator, and Sustainer of the universe. Yet this creation of the Father is through the Son and by the Holy Spirit."[6]

This observation of subordination within the triune co-equal Godhead is well established in Scripture. For example, Jesus Christ's works and words during his earthly ministry did not originate from him (Christ), but rather, from the Father (**John 5:19**; **14:10**). The Holy Spirit does not speak of himself, but rather glorifies Christ (**John 16:13-15**). It is God the Father who gives the kingdoms of the world to Christ after he (Jesus) won them through his work at Calvary and the resurrection (**Matthew 28:18**; **Revelation 11:15**). At the culmination of the Age, it is Jesus who will present us to the Father (**Jude 24**). All things will be put by the Father under Christ's authority, and yet within the triunity of the Godhead, Christ will remain subject unto the Father (**1 Corinthians 15:24-28**).

B. Creation of the Heavens

Not only is God 'triune,' but His works also reflect a three-fold aspect to His creativity. Though controversial in some of his conclusions, the late Reformed Christian teacher and numerologist Harold Camping affirmed a widely held view that Bible numbers have specific spiritual significance. He asserted that the number "3" in the Bible always speaks to, "the purpose of God."[7] It is quite possible that the three-dimensional aspect of God's creativity is to establish for us, in an unmistakable and unchangeable manner, His divine purposes.

There are many examples one could cite regarding God's three-phase approach to his creation, but even the heavens (plural) speak to this truth. The Bible speaks of a "third heaven" (**2 Corinthians 12:2**), this alluding to the fact that there must be two other heavens. From the earth's perspective there clearly are three heavens. The first heaven is our earth's atmosphere from whence we get the air we breathe, rainwater, climate, weather, and protection for the surface of the earth where we live. The second heaven is obviously outer space where the planets, solar systems and galaxies of our vast universe were placed. The third heaven referred to by the Apostle Paul is beyond the natural creation, in another dimension, as Renald Showers states, where "God dwells."[8]

In his work, *The Bible and Modern Science*, Christian scientist Henry M. Morris described the physical universe as a, "trinity of trinities."[9] Boa explains this statement as follows: "The main trinity consists of space, mass energy (matter), and time. Each of these elements is further divided into another trinity."[10] The three-dimensional sub-divisions are: Length, width and height for Space; energy, motion and phenomena for Matter; and past, present and future for Time.

C. Creation of Matter

A close look at the physical world reflects God's three-dimensional approach to creation. In *Realm of the Universe*, an element of matter is scientifically defined by author George O. Abell as, "A substance that cannot be decomposed, by chemical means, into simpler substances."[11] It is the base elements that form the earth, sea, and sky. Their forms are solids, liquids, and gasses.

Stewart J. Inglis notes in his work, *Physics: An Ebb and Flow of Ideas*, that in the study of physics, Newton discerned and categorized three axioms, or laws of motion (for the sake of brevity not enumerated here), which form the basis for all "Newtonian mechanics."[12] Scientists have also discovered that there are three species of fundamental forces, each of successive strength: Gravitation, electromagnetic forces, and nuclear forces (in "weak" and "strong" modes).[13] In mathematics, triangulation[14] is an arithmetic geometric technique that has enabled investigators to plot and document crime scenes, civil engineers to survey exact distances of objects beyond their reach, and astronomers to accomplish accurate measurements of celestial bodies light years in distance from the earth.

These few scientific examples witness to God's divine wisdom in his choosing to utilize a three-dimensional approach to his creation. It is a reflection of Himself, in the form of 'general revelation,' so that we may recognize and appreciate the wonder of His glory.

Boa refers to the simplicity of water, an H_2O molecule composed of three atoms (two Hydrogen and one Oxygen), as a clear example of God's three-fold creationism that reflects His triune nature. Boa observed that:

> "Another 'three-in-one' illustration is water (H_2O). Water retains its chemical identity whether in the solid, gas, or liquid state. Given the proper temperature and pressure, there is also a *triple point* for H_2O. This is a condition under which ice, steam, and liquid water can coexist in equilibrium. The three phases are all H_2O, but they are distinct from one another."[15]

Renald Showers refers to the three living species of God's creation: man, animal (mammal) and fish, and "all the different kinds of life forms that exist in the heavens, the earth, and the sea,"[16] the three God-provided dwelling places for His created beings. Scientists at times categorize life forms differently, but still with three distinctions: Animals (including humans and fish), plant life, and, "a host of 'lesser' species (such as myriad forms of bacteria) that fall into neither one kingdom or the other."[17] Furthermore, Showers distinguishes three species of personal beings that exist in the universe: "divine, angelic, and human."[18]

In addition to God's physical creation of matter, we could cite additional observations where God chooses to operate with his created beings in threes. Consider the God-given Mosaic Law consisting of the Ten Commandments and a total of 614 laws. The 614 laws have been separated by Rabbis into three distinct categories; civil, ceremonial, and moral. Note also the three major Old Testament Covenants of God with man; the Abrahamic, Mosaic, and Davidic, which are all fulfilled by Jesus Christ in the New Testament covenant.

Our prayer life, if exercised appropriately, is actually accomplished in a three-dimensional manner. There seems to have risen a practice in the contemporary Christian church, in my view alarmingly incorrect, where we address our prayers to a specific Person of the triune Godhead, depending on the content of our prayer, as if each

Person of the Godhead has a particular portfolio of responsibilities. For example, if we have material needs, we might address the Father. If we desire salvation, we pray to the Son. If we seek strength to overcome a situation, we may call upon the Holy Spirit. It is very common these days to hear prayers, even from Pastors and supposedly learned Christian leaders, addressed directly to the Holy Spirit, or to Jesus with the concluding the petition statement being, "in Your name." I believe it is improper to pray individually to each Person of the Trinity as if we're petitioning three Gods. This mode of prayer is equally wrong when practiced by the opposite heretical error of "Modalism" (3rd Century theologian Sabellius' idea that our one God reveals Himself in three 'modes': Father, Son, *or* Holy Spirit), therefore suggesting we can pray to whichever manifested 'mode' we feel fits our particular need at the time! Our prayers, if uttered correctly, are to be singular, but three-dimensional, in the sense that we petition the Father, with the leading and enablement of the Holy Spirit, and in the name of Jesus the Son who provided us with the access to the Father.

Not only is our worship and reaching out to God by prayer accomplished in a three-dimensional manner, but it has been observed that to get our attention God sometimes deals with us in a triple-emphatic manner. In the Bible, both Old and New Testaments, God uses repetition for emphasis. In the *Holiness of God*, R.C. Sproul notes that, "On a handful of occasions the Bible repeats something to the third degree. To mention something three times in succession is to elevate it to the superlative degree, to attach to it emphasis of super importance."[19] Sproul goes on to cite the three "woes" of Revelation, and mentions "holiness" as the only attribute of God that is elevated by repetition to the third degree.

We might note additional triple-emphasis examples. Consider God's three-time calling of Samuel which resulted in nation-altering developments (**1 Samuel 3**). Or, when just prior to his crucifixion, Jesus prayed three times in the Garden of Gethsemane (**Matthew 26:36-46**). There were three crosses at Calvary, where our Lord hung between two sinners, one lost and one saved. Jesus was "three days and three nights in the heart of the earth," as a comparison to Jonah's three-day/night experience in the whale's belly, (**Matthew 12:40**). Peter's vision, repeated three times, opened the gateway for the salvation of Gentiles

(**Acts 10:1-11,18**). Paul also pleaded with God three times concerning his "thorn in the flesh" before he was satisfied with God's response for him (**2 Corinthians 12:7**).

Furthermore, there are more than coincidental references to the number "three" in Christ's ministry and miracles. At the risk of bordering on the controversy of numerology, which I do not wish to elaborate on or lend support to in this book, in a significant number of works and miracles accomplished by Jesus where we are provided numbers, they are divisible by three. Note for example that there were 12 baskets of loaves and fish fragments left over when Jesus miraculously multiplied them to feed the people. There were 153 fish caught when Jesus told Peter to cast his net on the right side of the boat. On the day of Pentecost, there were 120 in the upper room, and later three thousand souls were saved. Whether we can derive some deeper significance from these and other examples is not the focus of this book. But, as previously stated, we can safely concede that these references do often point towards a beneficial teaching regarding the "purpose" of God.

Finally, even the Evil One imitates God's three-dimensional strategies. Jonathan Cahn brilliantly identified Satan's "Dark Trinity" in his recent book *Return of the Gods*. In the Old Testament, the three false gods that in tangent plagued God's covenant people (Israel) the most, were Baal, Ashtoreth and Molech. In the end times, as foretold by Jesus, by the Apostles in their epistles, and detailed in Revelation, Satan (the "Dragon'), his Antichrist (the 'Beast'), and the 'False Prophet,' will all three be in full operation.

CHAPTER ONE ENDNOTES

[1] Kenneth Boa, *GOD, I Don't Understand*, (Wheaton: Victor Books, 1976), 42.

[2] William H. Hordern, *A Layman's Guide to Protestant Theology*, (New York: Macmillan Publishing, 1968), 17.

[3] Stan Rosenthal, *One God or Three?*, (Orlando: Zion's Hope, 1997), 11.

[4] Rosenthal, 12.

[5] Boa, 35.

[6] Boa, 38.

[7] Harold Camping, *1994?*, (New York: Vantage Press, 1992), 378, 484.

[8] Renald Showers, *Angels*, (Bellmawr, NJ: Friends of Israel, 1997), 119.

[9] Henry M. Morris, *The Bible and Modern Science*, (Chicago: Moody Press, 1951), 24.

[10] Boa, 40.

[11] George O. Abell, *Realm of the Universe*, (Philadelphia: Saunders College, 1980), 389.

[12] Stuart J. Inglis, *Physics: An Ebb and Flow of Ideas*, (New York: John Wiley & Sons, 1970), 90.

[13] Abell, 7-8.

[14] Abell, 207.

[15] Boa, 41.

[16] Showers, 18.

[17] Richard L. Scheffel, ed., *ABC's of Nature*, (Pleasantville, NY: Reader's Digest Assoc., 1984), 158.

[18] Showers, 19.

[19] R.C. Sproul, *The Holiness of God*, (Wheaton: Tyndale House, 1985), 39-40.

CHAPTER 2
THE TRICHOTOMY OF MAN

"So God created man in his own image, in the image of God created he him; male and female created he them."
Genesis 1:27

Before moving on, we must recognize that God created us in His image so that we may be enabled to have fellowship with Him (**1 Corinthians 1:9**).[1] God wants us to have fellowship and relationship with Him in this life because He desires for us to be ultimately and eternally transformed into the image of His Son (**Romans 8:29a; 1 John 3:2; Philippians 3:21**).[2] We have no ability in and of ourselves to be reconciled to God. By nature, because of our sin, we are enemies of God. It is God himself, who by grace, through Jesus Christ, reconciles us unto Himself (**Romans 5:10**)![3]

The more man estranges himself from God, the more insanely depraved his sinful nature becomes. Today's largely Godless culture irrationally rejects God in all matters of life. For example, we insist on believing in 'science,' and without question embrace dubious human science such as "climate change," and not sin, as being the cause of epidemics, psychological illnesses, calamities, social and economic turmoil, wars, etc. Yet, for all of our scientific intellectual advances we seem to be having trouble understanding and accepting the established basic concepts of biology. In blind stubborn rebellion against God, we insist we cannot be tied down to an 'assigned' birth gender, and can't even define what a 'woman' is. We can't bring ourselves to believe the unborn fetus in the womb is a precious human life. We, by nature as enemies of God, are in desperate need of His transformation and reconciliation by grace through Christ.

An understanding of the relationship we desperately need with God is critical for the ability to make sense of everything we've discussed thus far, and what will be discussed in the rest of this book. The Westminster Shorter Catechism declares in its very first statement that, "The chief end of man is to glorify God, and to enjoy Him forever."[4] A basic understanding of the triune essence of God, the trichotomy of man, and the many three-fold works of God is necessary for the proper glorification of God and is useful in appreciating the message of *Soul Baptism*.

A. Spirit, Soul, and Body: 3 Christian Baptisms

We have already laid significant groundwork justifying the trichotomous essence of man. We've concluded that although man's wisdom is often inadequate to discern this three-fold distinction, it is through the revelation of God's Word that we find rest in these truths; i.e., "For the word of God *is* quick, and powerful, and sharper than any two-edged sword, piercing even to the dividing asunder of soul and spirit..." (**Hebrews 4:12a**).

In the pages ahead we shall explore further the underlying concepts of salvation that relate to the three-dimensional emphasis of this book. But here, let's discuss an interesting observation regarding the 'three' Christian baptisms. At first glance, a Bible-familiar reader may recoil at this concept of "three baptisms," reciting the scripture that comes immediately to mind declaring that there is but "one baptism," (**Ephesians 4:5**).[5] There is indeed one baptism that results in salvation. But, when considering Christ's ordinance of water baptism, every understanding Christian will readily admit to at least two Christian baptisms. Neither the latter (water baptism), nor the third ("soul baptism"), lead to salvation. They are subsequent to the Spirit's baptism of regeneration unto salvation. Though this will be elaborated further in the succeeding chapters (esp. Chpt. 9), for the purposes of this chapter on the trichotomy of man, let me suggest that each one of the three baptisms I'm referring to relates primarily to, and with focus upon, either the spirit, the soul, or the body components of man. "Baptisms" is *plural* in **Hebrews 6:2**.

The Holy Spirit's baptism of regeneration unto salvation is the supernatural baptism of man's *spirit*, transforming it from its dead state to life, (**1 Corinthians 12:13; Ephesians 2:1,5**).[6] It is the "born-again" salvation experience. Though it is God who initiates, draws, convicts and convinces; it is man who by faith must believe and willingly receive this supernatural gift of God, (**John 3:15-16**).[7]

Water baptism (*not infant baptism*) is a willful outward representation testifying in witness to the inward supernatural work of salvation which was already accomplished in a believer's spirit by the Spirit of God, unto salvation. It symbolizes our identification to Christ's death and resurrection. Water baptism is to be done subsequent to conversion and it is purely external. It is the *body* that is submersed and gets wet. It is a properly authorized minister who normally administers water baptism to a willing candidate who in obedience to God's Word, submits to Christ's command, (**Romans 6:4; Matthew 28:19**).[8] Notice that even the formula for water baptism is triangulated, instructing Christian ministers to baptize in the name of the "Father, Son, and Holy Spirit."

The "soul baptism" is the third baptism. As the term implies it is a baptism, or immersion of God's Spirit, upon the *soul* of man, in order to comfort and empower, or enable him for an enhanced Christian walk and service. It is commonly referred to in the New Testament as the "baptism with the Holy Spirit." John the Baptist, referring to Jesus Christ, said, "*I indeed have baptized you with water: but he shall baptize you with the Holy Ghost,*" (**Mark 1:8**). This baptism fortifies the inner, immaterial part of man. Not the spirit of converted man (*which has already been made alive*), but the soul component of man. The intellect, emotions and will of man are affected, so that his soul is spiritually reinvigorated via the illumination of the mind (**Matthew 10:20**), comfort in the emotions (**John 14:18,26**), and empowerment of the will (**Luke 24:49; Philippians 2:13**).[9] The candidate must be born again (**John 14:17**),[10] and like the other baptisms, he must believe and be willing to receive. Non-Pentecostal ministers and preachers are certainly anointed and empowered by God to fulfill their calling. But if we're true to God's Word, this third baptism is God's provision for that anointing of illumination and empowerment at an enhanced level beyond man's natural endowments.

B. God's Communication with Man

"God *is* a Spirit, and they that worship him must worship *him* in spirit and in truth" (**John 4:24**). Since God is a Spirit, and since He created man in His image as a spiritual being, it is logical that God would commune with man through his human spirit. In fact, God demands that we worship him with our spirit. He does not demand, sanction or receive carnal worship, nor soulish worship. Watchman Nee, in his translated-from-Chinese work entitled, *The Latent Power of the Soul,* makes clear distinction between a minister's use of "soulical or spiritual power." Nee explained that, "We need to discern… if a person's power is psychical or spiritual."[11]

That God indeed communicates with man needs clarification. There are those that claim to receive frequent messages and even regularly engage in two-way conversation with God. Often we may find that this dialogue is from impressions of the soul, through the mind or emotions, and is suspect. John MacArthur, an ardent anti-charismatic who I admire, but with whom I can't always agree, describes in his book *Charismatic Chaos* the soulical sequence this way, "…the worshiper would get into a state where his mind would go into neutral and his emotions would take over. The intellect and conscience would give way to passion, sentiment, and emotion."[12]

When God communes with man it is generally through his spirit. When God by His Spirit brings to our minds illumination or a remembrance of things we have learned of Him, it is through the open gateway of the regenerated spirit. When He brings comfort to our distressed hearts or emboldens our will, it again is through the gateway of our quickened spirit.

Jesus said, "*It is the spirit that quickeneth; the flesh profiteth nothing: the words that I speak unto you, they are spirit, and they are life,*" (**John 6:63**). Even though in the Authorized Version the word "spirit" in the first section of this verse in not capitalized, many commentators on this verse assume the word "spirit" refers to the Holy Spirit who "quickens," or makes alive. However, this passage can be properly understood to mean that it is the human spirit which becomes alive (*quickeneth*) by the work of the Spirit, as referred to in contrast to the flesh. It would not make sense to compare the Holy Spirit with man's flesh. Even Donald Guthrie, one of those commentators who takes the "Spirit" view, (i.e., that Jesus is referring to the Holy Spirit), concedes that, "It is possible that the word *pneuma* in John 6:63 may refer to the human spirit (as RSV supposes)."[13] The point being, that God does not minister to man's flesh in terms of redemption. God deals with the spirit of man as He draws him unto Himself. The soul and the flesh follow as man gives way to the tug in his spirit by God's Spirit.

In writing to the Romans, the Apostle Paul concurs with this soteriological concept that the soul and flesh follow behind God's moving on man's spirit, when he states, "That if thou shalt confess with thy mouth the Lord Jesus, and shalt believe in thine heart that God hath raised him from the dead, thou shalt be saved," (**Romans 10:9**). When God moves upon man's spirit, as if stirring the dead spirit out of slumber, it is man's soul which must consciously respond and the flesh must obey. Bible commentator Matthew Henry, in his exposition of **Romans 10:9** states, "We must devote, dedicate, and give up to God, our souls and our bodies; our souls in believing with the heart, and our bodies in confessing with the mouth."[14]

Once man becomes "born again," God continues to stir his spirit as He communes with him. The prophet Jeremiah described his intense stirring this way, "*Then I said, I will not make mention of him, nor speak any more in his name. But his word was in my heart as a burning fire shut up in my bones, and I was weary with forbearing, and I could not stay,*" (**Jeremiah 20:9**). Jeremiah is describing how God's stirring of his innermost spirit affected his soul and flesh. He described these in terms of "heart" and "bones." God's intense tugging at his spirit so wearied the resistance of his soul and even affected him physically, that Jeremiah had to give in and obey God's calling to minister His Word. Though Jeremiah was an Old Testament prophet, God deals with man similarly in the New Testament era.

In the New Testament, the ascended Jesus described Saul's threshold struggle to conversion as it being hard for him to "*kick against the pricks,"* (**Acts 9:5**). Similarly, later when the now converted Paul and his companions in ministry intended to proceed to Asia, they *"were forbidden of the Holy Ghost,"* and *"the Spirit suffered them not"* to go (**Acts 16:6-7**). In both incidents Saul/Paul was intent on proceeding as he had contemplated in his mind, emotions, and will. But God dealt with his spirit, leading him to where He wanted his servant to go. As Saul/Paul conceded he found physical restoration, and rest in his soul with the spiritual comfort and blessing of God.

C. Satan's Communication with Man

Un-regenerated man's spirit is 'dead,' or in a dormant state. Satan can only communicate, lure, impress, or bind the unsaved man via his soul or body. There are many accounts in the Gospels of men and women who Jesus delivered, who had been afflicted in their souls and/or bodies by Satan and his demons. The synagogue demoniac (**Luke 4:33-36**), the dumb demoniac (**Matthew 9:32-35**), the Gadarene demoniacs (**Mark 5:1-20**), and the demon-possessed boy (**Matthew 17:14-18**), are but a few examples.

Merrill Unger, in his book, *Demons in the World Today*, describes demon possession as one who is, "subject to periodic attacks by one or more inhabiting demons, who derange them physically and mentally during the seizure."[15] Unger expands on his description of the effects of demon possession on the soul and physical body of the victim by noting that, "The chief characteristic of demon possession or demonomania is the automatic projection of a new personality in the victim."[16] Regarding the physical affect on the victim's body, Unger says:

> "The abnormal or demonized stages can last a few minutes or several days. Sometimes the attacks are mild; sometimes they are violent. If they are frequent and violent, the health of the subject suffers."[17]

A lesser level of demon intrusion than possession, is demon influence or oppression. Satan uses demons to tempt and/or oppress men's souls in order to oppose and attempt to thwart the works of God on the earth, by causing men to disobey God and to derail God's plans. Happily, regenerated men have spiritual protection in that their spirits have been quickened and are indwelt by the Holy Spirit. Saved man can be engaged, but not dominated by demons. In responding to the question of "What Demons Can Do to People," Unger states:

"The character of demons reveals what they can do to their victims. Invisible, extremely intelligent, strong, and totally depraved personalities can do a great deal of harm to the unregenerate person, leading him into evil (**Ephesians 2:2-3**). As believers it is good to know that God is for us and that Christ's victory is complete (**Colossians 1:13**). He protects us from evil. The healthy Christian will never suffer from occult domination."[18]

The sum of this thought is that Satan communes, affects, and attempts to control man through his soul and the physical affliction of his body. The gateway of man's spirit is always closed to Satan because unregenerate man's spirit is dead, and because regenerate man's spirit is inaccessible by virtue of it having been made alive in Christ and indwelt by the Spirit.

This is why it is crucial that our offering of worship to God initiates from our spirit. Unregenerate man can seek God and pray, but he cannot acceptably worship. Regenerate man must worship "*in spirit and in truth*" (**John 4:24**). Soulish or carnal worship is an offense to God. Worship is not only the expressions of praise to God in a church setting, but one's heart attitude in the manner in which he lives his life before God.

In condemning the Christian's "soulish" lifestyle, Andrew Strom refers to a section in Volume 1-3 of Watchman Nee's work entitled *The Spiritual Man*, and states as follows:

"Surely Watchman Nee's words are tragically true, not only of many Christians today, but sadly of many leaders also: 'The corrupted old man in the believer has died but his soul remains the power behind his walk. On the one hand the sinful nature has been drastically touched but on the other hand the self life still persists and therefore cannot escape being soulish... To depend upon the soul life to carry out the wish of the spirit is to use natural (or human) force to accomplish supernatural (or divine) goodness. This is simply trying to fulfill God's demand with self-strength... Few are those disposed honestly to acknowledge their weakness and incapability and to lean utterly upon God. Who will confess his uselessness if he has not been humbled by the grace of God? Man takes pride in his prowess... He does not understand that however good to the human outlook his efforts may appear to be, they can never please God... He fails miserably to be spiritual and continues to abide in the soul.'"[19]

In his work, *The Normal Christian Life*, Watchman Nee expands on regenerated man's dilemma: the struggle in the human mind between his regenerated spirit and his carnal flesh. Nee states:

"I may have by nature a keen mind. Before my new birth I had it naturally, as something developed from my natural birth. But the trouble arises here. I become converted, I am born anew, a deep work is affected in my spirit, an essential union has been wrought with the Father of our spirits. Thereafter there are in me two things: I have now a union with God that has been set up in my spirit, but at the same time I carry over with me something which I derive from my natural birth. Now what am I going to do about it?"[20]

Nee provides the answer to his own question by stating that living the normal Christian life includes the continued normal use of one's God-given intellectual functions. One must only steer his mind from one set of thoughts to another, such as from worldly distractions to the study and meditation of God's Word. God helps us by transforming our desires and changing our interests.

In condemning the Christian's fleshly lifestyle, David Wilkerson in his book entitled, *Set the Trumpet to Thy Mouth*, declares, "I believe in the grace of God, but I also believe in His government... It was grace that clothed Adam; it was government that drove him out of Eden."[21] What Wilkerson is declaring is that forgiveness for the truly repentant is always available, but that judgment from God is inevitable for those who think they can get away with worshipping God while dabbling in carnal sins. God's economy will not permit it. We are called to worship in "spirit and in truth."

It is my conclusion that soulish and carnal men (i.e., those who's wills are dominated by their intellect, feelings, or carnal desires) follow

Lucifer's pattern and will always draw attention to themselves, seeking their own glory rather than the glory that belongs to God. As a life-long Pentecostal during the second half of the Twentieth Century and now into the third decade of the Twenty-first Century, I have seen a definite shift within the Christian Church, across denominational lines. From practices that were once more God-centered, to those more human-centered. It's a trend apparent to me that even born-again Christians have in some instances become more soulish and carnal in their Christian-related activities and ministries.

Consider names for churches: Traditional church names of the past more often reflected a greater respect for God in that they focused on Him and His works. Sometimes contemporary church names seem to focus more on man and his activities. For example, common church names used to exalt the Head of the Church and very often included the words God, Christ or Christian, Trinity, Calvary, Redeemer, Gospel, and the like. A quick review of an area's "Yellow Pages" directory will show that more churches are now named in a manner that focuses more on us and our activities, using terms such as; Worship Center, Family Center, Faith, Praise, Fellowship, Life, Love, Victory, or other catchy names designed to emphasize the congregation's supposed character rather than the character of God. Of course, our culture as a whole reflects a similar triviality. For example, while we used to select names for our children that had some family significance or reflection of our faith and values, today many parents select untraditional catchy names that sound cute or are just uniquely different from the norm.

Consider church worship services: Traditional hymns and songs, though at times over-emphasizing God's transcendence over His immanence, tended to be rich in doctrine, exalting God, proclaiming His divine attributes and His works. Quite often however, contemporary lyrics may over-emphasize God's immanence, tending to be shallower, and self-centered, focusing more on our act of worship, our feelings, our needs, our benefits, and our blessings. Likewise, lyrics that romanticize our relationship with Christ, with statements alluding to 'falling in love with Him,' or physically being 'embraced' by Him, can be misdirected and *soulish*. Music arrangements that aim to stimulate the senses rather than the spirit can be *carnal*. Mimicking the world, musical performances in church have at times been louder and louder, with special effects and beats that move the flesh rather than the spirit of man. Evangelist Mario Murillo quips regarding some of the carnal and sensational ministry techniques, describing them as, "big screens, skinny jeans, and fog machines."

While there is room for various ministry styles that are meaningful to the culture, worshipping "*in spirit and in truth*" is what's ultimately required. There's a difference between a church 'song service' and true 'worship.' Even this can be analyzed in a three-dimensional manner: We can sing songs that focus on **our** needs and benefits to make us feel better, and that can be *good*. We can sing **about** Him, which is *better*. Or we can sing **to** Him, combining praise, adoration, and thanksgiving, which is the *best* worship. So, true excellence in worship is found when our songs, sung to Him from the depths of our spirit, encompass **all three** dimensions; thanksgiving for **our** blessings, praise for His glorious works that are **about** Him, and glorification of His Person **to** him!

The conduct of church services and the preaching of the Word also seemed in the past to be more reverent and expository. You'd come away feeling like you've been spiritually nourished, having sensed the presence of our holy God, and evidencing having "*been with Jesus*," (**Acts 4:13**). Over time it has been my observation that messages from the pulpit are at times now more timid, perhaps crafted to be more entertainment-oriented, seeker-friendly, unoffensive, even with over-reliance on special mood effects, multi-media and the arts, in order to draw people by making them comfortable, stirring the senses, and entertaining them with shallow preaching riddled with corny one-liners, offering mainly self-help principles with a reluctance to confront and offer the remedy for sin.

None of this is to suggest that we ought not to use the latest technologies, avoid humor to convey important truths, or fail to adjust our methods in order to be relevant and effective in better communicating to our culture. But if the Christian man becomes more soulish and carnal, he opens the gateway for Satan-inspired error. If we discipline ourselves to be spiritual worshippers, we will become more sensitive to the Holy Spirit and the discerning of God's Word in how we ought to properly conduct ourselves in our ministries and the worship of God. This is why the Apostle Paul exhorted the Galatians to *"Walk in the Spirit, and ye shall not fulfill the lust of the flesh,"* (**Galatians 5:16**). We ought to proclaim the gospel in an effective manner and not blindly rely on either what may have worked in generations past, nor on new sensational or unoffensive gimmicks that artificially create a desired emotional atmosphere, or otherwise camouflage who God is and who we are (*or are to be*) in Christ. The only way I know to accomplish that effectiveness is by the prayerful reliance on the power of the Holy Spirit.

CHAPTER TWO ENDNOTES

[1] *"God is faithful, by whom ye were called unto the fellowship of his Son Jesus Christ our Lord,"* (**1 Corinthians 1:9**).

[2] *"For whom he did foreknow, he also did predestinate to be conformed to the image of his Son…"* (**Romans 8:29a**); *"Beloved, now we are the sons of God, but it doth not yet appear what we shall be: but we know that, when he shall appear, we shall be like him; for we shall see him as he is,"* (**1 John 3:2**); *"(Jesus Christ) Who shall change our vile body, that it may be fashioned like unto his glorious body, according to the working whereby he is able even to subdue all things unto himself,"* (**Philippians 3:21**).

[3] *"For if, when we were enemies, we were reconciled to God by the death of his Son, much more, being reconciled, we shall be saved by his life,"* (**Romans 5:10**).

[4] *The Westminster Shorter Catechism,* by the Assembly of the Divines at Westminster, Church of Scotland, 1648.

[5] *"One Lord, one faith, one baptism,"* (**Ephesians 4:5**).

[6] *"For by one Spirit are we all baptized into one body, whether we be Jews or Gentiles, whether we be bond or free; and have all been made to drink into one Spirit,"* (**1 Corinthians 12:13**); *"And you hath he quickened who were dead in trespasses and sins; Even when we were dead in sins, hath quickened us together with Christ, [by grace are ye saved],"* (**Ephesians 2:1,5**).

[7] *"For God so loved the world, that he gave his only begotten Son, that whosoever believeth in him should not perish, but have everlasting life,"* (**John 3:16**).

[8] *"Therefore we are buried with him by baptism into death: that like as Christ was raised up from the dead by the glory of the Father, even so we also should walk in newness of life,"* (**Romans 6:4**); *"Go ye therefore, and teach all nations, baptizing them in the name of the Father, and of the Son, and of the Holy Ghost,"* (**Matthew 28:19**).

[9] Mind – *"For it is not ye that speak, but the Spirit of your Father which speaketh in you,"* (**Matthew 10:20**); Emotions – *"I will not leave you comfortless: I will come to you; But when the Comforter, which is the*

Holy Ghost, whom the Father will send in my name, he shall teach you all things, and bring all things to your remembrance, whatsoever I have said unto you," (**John 14:18, 26**); Will – *"And, behold, I send the promise of my Father upon you: but tarry ye in the city of Jerusalem, until ye be endued with power from on high,"* (**Luke 24:49**), *"For it is God which worketh in you both to will and to do of his good pleasure,"* (**Philippians 2:13**)

[10] *"Even the Spirit of truth; whom the world cannot receive, because it seeth him not, neither knoweth him: but ye know him; for he dwelleth with you, and shall be in you,"* (**John 14:17**).

[11] Watchman Nee, *The Latent Power of the Soul*, (New York: Christian Fellowship Publishers, 1972), 49.

[12] John F. MacArthur, Jr., *Charismatic Chaos*, (Grand Rapids: Zondervan, 1992), 164.

[13] Donald Guthrie, *New Testament Theology*, (Downers Grove, IL: Inter-Varsity Press, 1981), 528.

[14] Matthew Henry, *Matthew Henry Commentary on the Holy Bible, Vol. 3*, (Nashville: Royal Publishers, 1979), Epistles, 52.

[15] Merrill Unger, *Demons in the World Today*, (Wheaton: Tyndale House, 1971), 139.

[16] Unger, 141-142.

[17] Unger, 141.

[18] Unger, 32.

[19] Andrew Strom, *Great Healing Revivalists: How God's Power Came*, (c.1996), www.christianword.org/revival/healing/html.

[20] Watchman Nee, *The Normal Christian Life*, (Wheaton: Tyndale House, 1983), 230.

[21] David Wilkerson, *Set the Trumpet to Thy Mouth*, (Lindale, TX: World Challenge, 1985), 47-48.

Chapter 3
The Three Spheres Of
Spiritual Warfare

"And you hath he quickened, who were dead in trespasses and sins;
Wherein in time past ye walked according to the course of this
<u>world</u>, according to the <u>prince of the power of the air</u>,
the spirit that now worketh in the children of disobedience:
Among whom also we all had our conversation in times past in the
<u>lusts of our flesh</u>,
fulfilling the desires of the flesh and of the mind;
and were by nature the children of wrath, even as others."
Ephesians 2:1-3

Our sin problem produces spiritual death and is also three-dimensional. We find there are three spheres or battlefronts wherein we engage in spiritual warfare. As underlined in the above scripture, they are: <u>Satan</u>, this <u>world system</u>, and our <u>flesh</u>. Satan's attack strategies are against our <u>spirit</u>, our <u>souls</u>, and our <u>bodies</u>.

Jesus' parable of the Sower and Soils, as recorded in **Matthew 13:1-23**, **Mark 4:1-20**, and **Luke 8:5-15**, provides an illustration of these three spheres of spiritual warfare. In that parable, Jesus tells of a sower (or preacher) who sows the "seeds" of God's Word on four different kinds of terrain: the <u>way side</u>, <u>upon rocks</u>, <u>among thorns</u>; and on <u>good soil</u>. The first three "bad" soils are descriptive of the three spheres of spiritual warfare.

A. Satan

In the parable of the Sower and Soils, Jesus indicates that Satan and his demons are depicted by the fowls of the air that devour the seeds falling on the way side (*the heart surfaces of the hearers*), lest they should believe and be saved. In this first sphere of conflict, the <u>spirit</u> of man is the target. Satan's goal is to prevent the quickening of man's dead spirit by stamping out any flicker of potential life as the Gospel stirs man, appealing for him to believe unto salvation.

Satan is the archenemy of our souls. His desire is to seek, steal, maim, kill, and destroy as many souls as he can. Thus, either rendering disabled those who already belong to God, or striving to solidify his possession of all those who are not yet redeemed. In effect, attempting to rob them from the reach of God who created them and sent His Son to die for them.

Jesus called Satan the original murderer and the father of lies (**John 8:44**), and it is through deceit that he seeks his prey. The Apostle Paul warns us that Satan is able to masquerade himself into a disguised angel of light, and into imposter ministers of righteousness, (**2 Corinthians 11:14-15**). Often Satan attempts to deceive Christians by counterfeiting the genuine things of God. He does so subtly by providing a comfortable and believable alternative that will result in the redirection of worship belonging to God, to himself. Satan accomplishes this by first minimizing sin and its consequences. Then by replacing the genuine with his false substitute. Next, he suggests redirected worship to the substitute. Finally, he utilizes human pride to convince man to make the shift, in effect resulting in Satan worship.

Consider how Satan deceived Eve: First, he minimized sin by questioning God's intent and by assuring her she wouldn't die. Secondly, he provided the alternative by offering what God had forbidden. Next, he tried to convince Eve to listen to him because God was holding out on her. He was finally able to convince Eve by tapping into her human pride, promising that if she obeyed him she would be as a 'goddess.'

This pattern is repeated time and time again. Some historical examples of how deception resulted in the abandonment of truth are found in these passages of Scripture:

1) In Genesis 4, <u>Cain</u>, after having had his parents' example of animal skins provided by God, indicating the requirement of shed blood and death to cover sins, proceeds to offer the first alternative "un-bloody" sacrifice. When extended an opportunity to offer an acceptable sacrifice, Cain refused, and with a hardened heart then slew Abel.

2) In Genesis 10, <u>Nimrod</u> desired an alternative way to reach heaven and become a "god." He pursued self-righteousness and self-deification. He began the worship of heavenly bodies (*astrology*) and the concept of self-deification, which plagued Israel all through its history. Nimrod's religion is still clearly seen today in the form of the "New Age"-type movements.

3) In Leviticus 10, <u>Nadab and Abihu</u>, legitimate priests and sons of Aaron, the very first High Priest, offered an alternative strange fire (*polluted worship*) before the Lord which He had not commanded. Their penalty was death.

4) In 1 Kings 12, <u>Jeroboam</u>, Israel's first king after the kingdom was split, established cult worship as an alternative to that which the people had been used to in Jerusalem. He did so to solidify his Northern Kingdom and prevent his people from migrating back to Judah. He accomplished this by creating an "official" priesthood and initiating a new style of worship, while being careful that it did not differ a great deal from that which they were familiar.

5) In 2 Kings 16, <u>Ahaz</u>, Judah's 12th king, duplicated a heathen altar and then burned traditional sacrifices on it. To ensure acceptance by the people, he was careful to temper his radicalism by utilizing the familiar Temple vessels, which he had rearranged to his liking.

All these are examples of how Satan, the enemy of our souls, seeks to deceive usin order to render us harm, and attempt to rob God of what belongs to Him. He does so convincingly, incrementally, and subtly. The New Testament Scriptures also warn us of the last days when false Christs and false prophets will actually be able to perform miraculous feats designed to deceive (*not successfully on the elect of God who He preserves* – **Matthew 24:24**). Again, this is not new! God warned His covenant people Israel of the existence of this miraculous level of deception in the Old Testament (**Deuteronomy 13:1-5**). The penalty for deception designed to lure people away from God was always death (**Deuteronomy 18:20**). <u>Satan</u> is our first sphere of spiritual warfare.

B. The World System

In the parable of the Sower and Soils, Jesus indicates that the cares and pleasures of this earthly life are as the thorns into which some of the sower's seed fell. The hearers initially responded to the Gospel, but got "choked" with the cares of this world and fell away, being rendered fruitless. In this second sphere of conflict, man's <u>soul</u> is the target. Satan, who rules the world system, uses all its vain attractions to pull on man's thoughts, his passions, and his determination of pursuits (his intellect, emotions, and will).

When we speak of the "world," the reader should not think of God's created earthly design or the beauty of nature. The biblical word "world" comes from the Greek term, *kosmos*, meaning, "an ordered system." It is not nature that's corrupt. It is this world system we live in that since the Fall became Satan's domain, which is ruled and influenced by him (**John 12:31, 14:30; Ephesians 2:2; 2 Corinthians 4:3-4**). That's why the Apostle John admonishes us to, "*Love not the world, neither the things that are in the world. If any man love the world, the love of the Father is not in him,*" (**1 John 2:15**).

This world (system) has been tried at Calvary and has been found guilty. It is condemned and under divine judgment. Similar to our American justice system, when a person is found guilty of a crime, there is a period of time that passes from the point of conviction to the point of sentence execution. This is where the world lies at this moment, and where God has placed the 'Church.' The world has already been declared guilty and it is now awaiting judgment. That judgment will be executed as part of the process surrounding the Second Coming of Jesus Christ. Meanwhile, although we're required to be good stewards as informed and responsible citizens, we were never called to salvage this condemned world. Rather, we are called out of it (**2 Corinthians 6:14-18**), and we're commissioned to urge others to escape its judgment as well!

We are the Church. The biblical word "church" comes from the Greek term *ekklesia*. Literally, *ek* means "out," and *klesia* means "to call." Therefore, the Church is an assembly of "called out" ones. The "church" is not the building, nor the organization. It is the people. It is composed of the ones who have heard and believed the Gospel, and heeded to the call to escape the coming judgment and "*come out from among them*" unto salvation (**2 Corinthians 6:17**). Again, the Apostle John reminds us that as Christians we are *in* the world but not *of* it (**John 17:11,16**). We have become the citizens of a "*better country*," (**Hebrews 11:16**). Salvation is not just 'accepting' Christ for the forgiveness of sins and avoidance of punishment. It is also a call to make Jesus Christ Lord of our lives.

This <u>world system</u> is our second sphere of spiritual warfare. Like the Rich Young Ruler (**Luke 18:18-23**), the cares of this world will keep the unsaved man from prioritizing the salvation of his soul. Like the Apostle Paul's comparison between the unmarried and the married (**1 Corinthians 7:32-33**), if not careful, the cares of this world will also distract the believer from his full potential of service to God. Like Daniel, the child of God must "purpose in his heart" that he will follow after the Lord, despite the world's lures, attractions, distractions, and opposition (**Daniel 1:8**).

C. The Flesh

In Jesus' parable of the Sower and Soils, the rocky terrain is a depiction of man's <u>flesh</u> (*the carnality of our physical bodies*). The initial response of joy upon hearing God's Word is quickly overwhelmed by the flesh's weakness in face of a subsequent temptation, tribulation, affliction, or persecution.

Because of man's sinful nature, he is susceptible to carnal weaknesses. Satan will use man's fleshly desires to keep him from either responding to the Gospel, or from thriving as God's child through affliction that keeps him from operating in the power of the Spirit.

Some of the most powerful fleshly temptations to man come from greed (**1 Timothy 6:10**), and from improper sexual desires. Even the world cites "money and women" as a quip for being man's greatest vulnerability! It is instructive that in the discussion of sexual sins, Wayde Goodall, in his book entitled *Why Great Man Fall*, concurs with Christian psychologist James Dobson in his identification of three levels of marital infidelity:

"Type 1: The one-night stand typified by David and Bathsheba (**2 Samuel 11**).

Type 2: The entangled affair similar to Samson and Delilah (**Judges 16**).

Type 3: Sexual addiction is illustrated by Eli's sons (**1 Samuel 2:22**)."[1]

It is apparent that the third realm of spiritual warfare is man's own <u>flesh</u>. But a major danger of carnal temptations is that fleshly appetites can grow. As Goodall's above-noted sequence describes, the intensity of carnal sin can be progressive from a brief satisfaction of an impulsive opportunity, to a depraved enslavement similar to a drug addict's inability to control his craving for more and more of that which satisfies less and less.

Scripture instructs us that the only way to fend off the power of the flesh's cravings is to be filled with and be walking "*in the Spirit*" (**Galatians 5:16-17**). The Apostle Paul's startling admission of his own fleshly struggles (**Romans 7:14-19**), reveals fully the intensity of the battle and that no one is immune to. In the next chapter (**Romans 8**), the Apostle Paul reminds the reader that those who are indwelled by the Spirit of God have a blessed hope, that even their mortal bodies will ultimately be transformed into a glorious state, no longer enslaved to sinful desires. Paul states, "*But if the Spirit of him that raised up Jesus from the dead dwell in you, he that raised up Christ from the dead shall also quicken your mortal bodies by his Spirit that dwelleth in you,*" (**Romans 8:11**).

It is faith in God and belief in His 'blessed hope' promises that has caused men to be single-minded enough to overcome the weaknesses of the flesh during times of intense temptations and afflictions. Consider the listed heroes and martyrs of **Hebrews 11**. Likewise, New Testament Christians were put to death for not renouncing their faith, even when faced with the most intense methods of coercion in the arenas run by the brutal Roman authorities. Like Stephen (**Acts 7:59-60**), they died with praise to God on their lips and expressions of prayer for their executioners (Jesus: **Luke 23:34**).

In man's spiritual warfare, the stony flesh is one of the three great battlefronts. Man's flesh, the seat of his five natural senses or receptors; (hearing, sight, taste, smell, and touch), wars against the spirit. When he had asked his closest disciples to watch and pray with him, only to then find them asleep, Jesus acknowledged this fact by stating, *"the spirit indeed is willing, but the flesh is weak"* (**Matthew 26:41**).

Prayer and fasting is an effective Christian discipline to strengthen the spirit and weaken the cravings of the flesh. Thankfully, the Spirit of God is ever ready to help us overcome as we yield ourselves to Him. And if we should fail, He is faithful and just to forgive us our trespasses and to cleanse from all unrighteousness (**1 John 1:9**).

CHAPTER THREE ENDNOTES

[1] Wayde Goodall, *Why Great Men Fall*, (Green Forest, AR: New Leaf Press, 2005), 62.

SECTION TWO:

GOD, MAN, AND PERSONAL SALVATION

CHAPTER 4
THE TRINITY AT WORK
IN MAN'S SALVATION

"Go ye therefore, and teach all nations, baptizing them in the
name of the Father, and of the Son, and of the Holy Ghost."
Matthew 28:19

We have established that God is a triune Being: One God, in the three Persons of the Father, Son, and Holy Spirit. The three Persons of the Trinity are co-equal, co-eternal, and co-involved in the regeneration of man, producing his salvation.

It is fitting that in the Great Commission (**Matthew 28:19**), the mandate is to go and baptize by water, in the authority of the Trinity (i.e., in the three names/Persons of the Godhead), Father, Son, and Holy Spirit. Regeneration is an act of grace. The salvation plan was ingeniously designed by the Father, provided for through the successful work of the Son, and effected by the quickening power of the Spirit.

A. Design of the Father

By his divine foreknowledge, God the Father knew of man's 'free-will' fall even before creation. Therefore, God foreordained a provision for man's salvation. He did so by divine mercy (not giving us the wrath we *do* deserve); and by grace (giving us blessings we *don't* deserve). God did this without obligation, and before man could even think to ask for it (**Romans 5:8**). God first proclaimed this provision in the **Genesis 3:15**[1] *protevangelium*, which Enns defines as, "the first announcement of the gospel in Scripture."[2] Enns further explained this protevangelium by asserting:

> "God initiates His redemptive program by promising a Savior to Adam and Eve. The promise anticipates Messiah's ultimate triumph over Satan, providing the basis for the restored kingdom… Satan would be dealt a destructive, head crushing blow."[3]

God's plan of salvation is ingenious, in that through an extraordinary divine act God defeated Satan's curse (of sin and death), and made available to sinful man a glorious and unmerited redemption (an eternal life of holiness). The plan was brilliant in that a holy and just God was able to redeem sinful man without being tainted by man's sin, without violating His justice, and by totally defeating every device of Satan. Probably the best known Bible passage to humanity captures the essence of this plan:

"For God so loved the world, that he gave his only begotten Son, that whosoever believeth in him should not perish, but have everlasting life," (**John 3:16**).

Other Scripture verses clearly depict the Father as the initiator of the gift of salvation to man. It is the Father from whom all blessings flow. Jesus said, *"No man can come to me, except the Father which hath sent me draw him,"* (**John 6:33a**). James said, *"Every good gift and every perfect gift is from above, and cometh down from the Father of lights, with whom is no variableness, neither shadow of turning. Of his own will begat he us with the word of truth, that we should be a kind of firstfruits of his creatures,"* (**James 1:17-19**).

B. Provided through the Son

In both the Old Testament and New Testament eras, salvation is provided by God for man in essentially the same manner. It is made available to man by God's grace, and it is made effectual in man through believing faith in God's provision.

In the Old Testament era, God provided a sacrificial system where man's sin could be covered. Man would be saved if he, by faith, appropriated God's provision through obedience by offering the required sacrifices in the precise manner prescribed. The ceremonial sacrifices had to be continually repeated so that man's subsequent, repetitive, and accumulating sins could continue to be covered. The sacrificial system was temporary, and it foreshadowed a type of something better to come that would be permanent without the requirement of continual repetition. That something better was the improved provision that would eventually be fulfilled in the Messiah.

The New Testament is that better provision. It is a new Covenant, wherein God procured a single, ultimate Messianic sacrifice, to end all other sacrifices, which would not merely cover man's sin temporarily, but would permanently take that sin away. To this point John the Baptist declared, "*Behold the Lamb of God, which taketh away the sin of the world*," (**John 1:29b**). That "Lamb of God" was not a four-legged animal, but it was Jesus Christ the Messiah, who *as* sacrificial Lamb, took upon himself our sins, carried them to the Cross where he paid our debt in full, and then rose victoriously to defeat the penalty of death. As our substitute, Jesus paid through his death, our penalty (the "wages") of sin (**Romans 6:23**).

In defining the doctrine of *substitution* in the context of Christology, Enns writes, "The emphasis of the New Testament, however, is that Christ died a substitutionary death on behalf of sinners. His death is also called *vicarious*, meaning, 'one in place of another'."[4] The single foundational backbone of Christianity is the essential doctrine of Jesus Christ's substitutionary provision. Without it, Christianity cannot stand. Jesus Christ, God's Son, is the Person by whom that provision of salvation was made.

We should emphasize that no other person could have substituted Jesus Christ as the Messiah. The Messiah had to be sinless, otherwise his death would have been for his own sins rather than for ours vicariously. Only Jesus had the credentials to be able to fulfill God the Father's plan and be the provider of man's salvation. This is so because Jesus was the 'God-man.' Jesus had to be fully God, lest man's original sin attach to him. But Jesus also had to be fully man, lest his sacrifice could not be legitimately vicarious for us. God answered this dilemma with what has been termed the doctrine of the "hypostatic union," (that Jesus was 100% God and 100% man – not a 'hybrid' 50-50).

Boa describes the essentiality of the hypostatic union. Citing many Bible passages that speak to Jesus' divine attributes and works, to include the power to forgive sins, Boa simply asserts, "the fact of Christ's full deity has clear biblical support."[5] Concerning Jesus' humanity, Boa makes clear that, "The substitutionary atonement requires that Jesus Christ must die as a man to bear judgment for the sins of all men… The Messiah could not have become the mediator between God and man apart from becoming the God-man by taking on human flesh."[6]

Salvation is therefore provided for us by God supernaturally, and it is provided exclusively through His Son. Sinful man generally doesn't like this exclusivity. Man wants choices and the ability to pick and choose his own method and level of salvation. This was evident in Cain's sin. Although Cain knew through the example of his parents, who's sins had been covered by the shedding of an animal's blood for the covering skins provided by God, he insisted on offering his own "unbloody" sacrifice (**Genesis 4:3**). In the New Testament, when preaching Jesus Christ to the Sanhedrin, the Apostle Peter affirmed this necessary exclusiveness by stating, *"Neither is there salvation in any other: for there is none other name under heaven given among men, whereby we must be saved,"* (**Acts 4:12**). Man must receive His forgiveness *and* submit to His Lordship.

C. Effected by the Spirit

If man's salvation plan was devised by the Father, and made possible through the Son, it is transacted by the Spirit. The Holy Spirit plays the essential role of effecting man's regeneration unto salvation. It is He who quickens our pre-regenerated dead spirits unto life. It was Jesus who proclaimed that, *"Except a man be born of water and of the Spirit, he cannot enter into the kingdom of God,"* (**John 3:5**).

In a display of the Trinitarian oneness of God, this New Testament Spirit-regeneration was launched per the Father's authority and design, by Jesus himself, as the first order of business, on the first day of that relatively brief 40-day period of time between Jesus' resurrection and his ascension. The Apostle John recorded the moment when Jesus, on the evening of Resurrection Sunday, appeared to His disciples and, *"breathed on them, and saith unto them, Receive ye the Holy Ghost,"* (**John 20:21-22**). This was the threshold moment of transition from the Old Testament salvation plan, to the better New Testament salvation plan designed to permanently replace the sacrificial Law of the Old. The day of Pentecost (**Acts 2**) was not that threshold "birthday of the Church" moment, as many suggest. Pentecost was the empowerment of the infant Church that was "born" when the resurrected Christ on Resurrection Day breathed on the disciples to receive the Holy Ghost.

From that moment of 'Christ's breathing' on his disciples, all existing, and subsequent believers in Jesus Christ as the Messiah, would become *born again* by the Spirit of God upon conversion. Every person saved since that **John 20:22** event, has been regenerated and baptized into the body of Christ by the Holy Spirit. The Apostle Paul affirmed this by the following saying, *"For by one Spirit are we all baptized into one body... and have been all made to drink into one Spirit,"* (**1 Corinthians 12:13**).

Alluding to this Spirit baptism unto salvation, R.C. Sproul states; "Without regeneration no one (*universal negative*) is able to enter the kingdom of God. There are no exceptions. It is impossible to enter God's kingdom without a rebirth."[7] It is evident then, that the complete Trinity is at work in achieving man's salvation. The Father devised, the Son provided, the Spirit executed.

CHAPTER FOUR ENDNOTES

[1] God to Satan: "*And I will put enmity between thee and the woman, and between thy seed and her seed; it shall bruise thy head, and thou shalt bruise his heel,*" (**Genesis 3:15**).

[2] Enns, 42.

[3] Enns, 42.

[4] Enns, 232.

[5] Boa, 22.

[6] Boa, 24.

[7] R.C. Sproul, *The Mystery of the Holy Spirit*, (Wheaton: Tyndale House, 1990), 95.

CHAPTER 5
THE TRICHOTOMY OF MAN AND SALVATION

"And the very God of peace sanctify you wholly; and I pray your whole <u>spirit</u> and <u>soul</u> and <u>body</u> be preserved blameless unto the coming of our Lord Jesus Christ."
1 Thessalonians 5:23

As a tripartite being, man needs complete salvation. The above scripture citing strongly suggests that the Apostle Paul's desire for the Thessalonian believers was for them to give attention not to neglect any aspect of their beings from achieving the full reward of God at Christ's Second coming.

Paul would not have been pleased if their salvation had been disjointed, in that, having their spirits quickened, they should neglect to discipline their souls or indulge in harmful fleshly activities, as a few years later he had to write to the Corinthians about. Paul's prayer for the Thessalonians, who were situated in the midst of a pagan society, was for them to be divinely assisted in their efforts and responsibility to preserve themselves from defilement so that Satan would not be given an opportunity to infiltrate, accuse, and disrupt the church at Thessalonica.

Our salvation affects every dimension of our being. Our spirits, souls, and bodies.

The following sections discuss this in each component of our beings.

A. Regeneration of Man's Spirit

Salvation begins when the Spirit of God causes us to become born-again by the quickening of our human spirit. Our spirit was dead (*separated and out of fellowship with God*), but upon regeneration is made alive (*in active fellowship with God*). The conversion process is initiated by God who convicts us of our sins and draws us unto Himself while offering a loving redemption. The proper salvation-producing response to that conviction is by faith, and three-fold: Recognition and repentance of sin, trust in Jesus Christ's ability to save, and complete abandonment to Him by faith (**Mark 1:15**). All three are required for the Holy Spirit to accomplish his work of regeneration. The Apostle Paul declares the result; "*Therefore if any man be in Christ, he is a new creature: old things are passed away; behold all things are become new,*" (**2 Corinthians 5:17**).

The questions that have over the centuries pitted Christian theologians against each other are, how salvation is attained, and whether it is possible for one who's spirit has been regenerated to enter into circumstances where he can "lose" his salvation. Basically, there are two opposing camps related to this discussion: The "Calvinists" are adamant in their belief that once a predestined individual is "born-again," he is eternally secure and can under no circumstances even remotely endanger his salvation. "Arminianists" argue that a free-will born-again individual who abandons the Christian walk and entangles himself again in a sinful lifestyle without repentance can reach a danger zone where he finds himself in real risk of forfeiting his salvation, because God cannot be mocked (**Hebrews 6:4-6; Galatians 6:7**).

"**Calvinism**" is a term derived from the name of its founder. "John Calvin (1509-1564) *was a* French Protestant reformer"[1] who emphasized God's sovereignty and predestination, resulting in the doctrine of "eternal security… associated with the perseverance of the saints."[2] Eternal security based on election is the most well known final conclusion in Calvin's system of theology. In simplified terms, the acronym "T.U.L.I.P." highlights the five tenets of Calvinism. Enns lists them as follows:

> "Five positive statements that summarize Calvinism were set forth at the Synod of Dort: 1) Total depravity of man; 2) Unconditional election to salvation; 3) Limited atonement (for the elect only); 4) Irresistible grace; 5) Perseverance of the saints."[3]

The "TULIP" acronym is also used by Calvinists to show the Trinity's work in transforming an elected sinful man unto salvation:

<u>Total Depravity</u> = Depicts man apart from God;

<u>Unconditional Election</u> = Man is elected (*predestined to salvation*) by the **Father**; <u>Limited Atonement</u> = The **Son**'s atoning work for elected man's salvation; <u>Irresistible grace</u> = The **Holy Spirit**'s application of salvation to elected man; and <u>Perseverance of the Saints</u> = Elected man living out his salvation.

"**Arminianism**" is a term derived from the name of its founder. Trained as a Calvinist who came to see the 'error' of Calvin's way, "Jacobus Arminius (1559-1609) *was a* Dutch theologian; founder of an anti-Calvinist Reformed theology."[4] Enns recounts Arminius' rethinking of Calvinism as follows:

> "Although Arminius began as a strict Calvinist (he had studied under Beza, Calvin's son-in-law, in Geneva), in defending Calvinism against Koornheert, he believed his opponent more ably defended his views. This defeat led Arminius to reject Calvinism"[5]

In succinct terms, theologian Herbert Lockyer describes those who subscribe to Arminianism as they who believe in a *conditional election*, which is "dependent on… *an individual's* …own steadfastness and diligence… *able to* …forfeit the gift of life by backsliding and apostasy."[6] In response to Calvin's "5 Points," Arminius also put forth his "Five Articles." Paul Enns summarizes them as follows:

"Major theological emphases of Arminianism are: conditional election based on the foreknowledge of God; God's grace can be resisted; Christ's atonement was universal; man has a free will and through prevenient grace can cooperate with God in salvation; the believer may lose his salvation."[7]

Both positions can be said to contain partial truths and partial errors! The most difficult principles of Calvinism are 'Unconditional Election' (*predestination*), 'Limited Atonement' (*Christ died for the 'elect' only*), and 'Irresistible Grace' (*elected man's inability to resist God's call to salvation*). The stronger points of Arminianism are 'conditional' election (*man must be willing to receive God's salvation*), the universality of Christ's Atonement (*Christ's sacrifice was sufficient for all*), and 'Prevenient' (*or enabling*) grace. God gives to every man the faith capability to believe, but it is not 'irresistible,' it must be volitionally exercised and is necessary as a 'condition' for salvation (**Hebrews 4:2**). The weakest principle of Arminianism is the potential for 'Loss' of one's salvation. The totality of Bible theology reveals quite clearly that God offers salvation to "*whosoever will*," because Christ's atonement is sufficient for every sin of every man in every generation (**John 3:15-16; Rev. 22:17; 1 John 2:1-2**). It is also clear that our salvation was provided solely by God without any contribution from man, and that we are both preserved and completely safe in the hands of God (**John 10:27-30**).

Calvinists will cite **John 6:37**, "*All that the Father giveth me shall come to me; and him that cometh to me I will in no wise cast out*," and **6:45b**, "*…Every man therefore that hath heard, and hath learned of the Father, cometh to me*," as a doctrinal 'closed-loop' in support of Calvinism's three more difficult principles. It's true that no person can come to the Father except through the gateway of the Son (**John 14:6**), and no one can be drawn to the Son except by the Father (**John 6:44**). But even in these of the 'strongest' passages used to support Calvinism's central points in their interpretation of sovereignty, it's clear that the ones the Father gives the Son are those who have both "*heard*" and "*learned*." That is indeed a 'closed loop' in terms of access, entry, and resulting 'eternal security' (**John 10:28-29**). But it's not one that overrides man's God-given free will. "*Hearers*" must follow through with *receiving* by faith (i.e., to "*learn*" by actually experiencing willfully after understanding) in order to attain (**Romans 2:13**; **James 1:22**).

I very much respect the Reformed believers' intellect, logic, and historical contributions. But while the Calvinistic T.U.L.I.P.'s first principle, "T" (the Total Depravity of man), at first glance sounds acceptable, it launches the whole Calvinistic system of theology into a doctrinal field beyond what most believers can reasonably concur with. Most will agree that man is utterly helpless in remedying his own depraved sinfulness. Man is in complete need of God's provision for redemption, provided only through Christ. But Calvinism's first point demands that unsaved people are 'totally depraved' in the sense of, and to the extent that, they have absolutely no spiritual conscience or faith-capability to be able to believe at all! They require God to have preselected an unsaved person, then tinker with his will, so that the individual is then infused by God with an irresistible compulsion to believe, so that he can no longer not believe, and therefore becomes saved. This is indeed problematic because it goes beyond the apparent teaching of many passages of Scripture! For Calvinism to then stand, what appears to be the Biblical order of events leading to salvation must be reversed. Instead of regeneration being received by faith in response to hearing the convicting Word (**Romans 10:17**), the Calvinist must argue that saving faith is given to man only <u>after</u> he is regenerated because he is incapable of any measure of belief beforehand.

On the Ligonier Ministries website (*https://www.ligonier.org/posts/regeneration-precedes-faith*), The late Presbyterian Pastor, RC Sproul, a champion of Calvinism, insists that, "Regeneration precedes faith." He's quoted as explaining it this way:

> "When we talk about regeneration preceding faith, this means that before a person exercises saving faith, before they believe in Christ, before that individual exercises his or her will to embrace Christ, God must do something for them and in them so that faith can be exercised. It is not that the Holy Spirit drags people kicking and screaming against their will to come to Christ. The Holy Spirit changes the inclination and disposition of our hearts so that, while we were previously unwilling to embrace Christ, now we are willing – and more than willing.

Indeed, we aren't dragged to Christ; we run to Christ, and we embrace Him joyfully because the Spirit has changed our hearts. The heart is no longer a heart of stone, impervious to the commands of God and to the invitations of the gospel."

Of course, there are elements of truth in the above statement regarding how God's love affects men's stony hearts, but **Romans 12:3** clearly teaches that God has given, "*to every man the measure of faith.*" This suggests that to everyone who was ever born, God has already instilled a measure of faith-capability for which he is responsible. It is a capacity to believe, which is sufficient in every person, in response to the Father's drawing and Spirit's work, to exercise unto salvation, and to also thereafter exercise and build up towards the fulfillment of whatever call of God to service is placed on his life. God is the original provider of man's faith, but man must be willing exercise it in response to God's drawing and in obedience to His leading. Man is capable of resisting God's drawing (**Acts 7:51**), and of misdirecting his God-given faith by applying it onto Satan's lies (**Genesis 3:4-5**; **John 8:44**; **2 Thessalonians 2:9-10**). In **2 Thessalonians 3:2**, Paul says *"for all men have not faith."* He's referring to those who refuse to exercise their faith unto God due to unbelief (**Romans 3:3**). For 'believing faith' to be truly valid, it must be truly volitional!

For example, God has created each of us with a full set of physical muscles. The one who exercises his muscles increases strength, but the one who doesn't, remains weaker than what his potential might have been. In His omniscient foreknowledge, God already knows who will exercise his faith and so predestines an escape pathway for him to willingly be able to follow. Initial belief leads to salvation, and subsequent obedience results in Christ's rewards (**2 Corinthians 5:10**). But the free unmanipulated exercise of faith is required for the relationship between God and man to be genuine and meaningful!

To support the doctrine of *sovereign predestination*, Calvinists elevate the Apostle Paul's epistles above the others, citing Romans 9 and the epistle to the Ephesians. It can be safely argued that when Paul quoted **Malachi 1:2-3** in **Romans 9:13**, that God loved Jacob over Esau, it was based on God's *foreknowledge* (**Romans 8:29**) of what Esau would choose to do in despising his birthright (**Genesis 25:34**). But

Calvinists then point to **Ephesians 1:4** "*He hath chosen us…before the foundation of the world*"; **1:5** "*Having predestinated us unto the adoption of children…according to the good pleasure of his will*"; **1:11** "*we have obtained an inheritance, being predestinated according to the purpose of him who worketh all things after the counsel of his own will.*" But Paul's central message to the Ephesians was <u>NOT</u> *individual predestination*! He was clearly revealing the previously hidden "*mystery,*" that before the foundations of the world God had *predestinated Gentiles* to one day become fellow heirs with His covenant people, *Israel.* This is repeatedly stated in **Ephesians 1:10** "*That in the dispensation of the fulness of times he might gather together in one all things in Christ*"; **1:13-19** "*But now in Christ Jesus ye who sometimes were far off are made nigh by the blood of Christ*"…"*he is our peace, who hath made both one*"…"*to make in himself of twain one new man*"…"*that he might reconcile both unto God in one body by the cross*"…"*And came and preached peace to you which were afar off* (Gentiles), *and to them that were nigh* (Israel)"…"*For through him we both have access by one Spirit unto the Father*"…"*Now therefore ye are no more strangers and foreigners, but fellow-citizens with the saints, and of the household of God.*" **2:22** "*In whom ye also are builded together for an habitation of God through the Spirit.*" **3:6** (the 'mystery') "*That the Gentiles should be fellow-heirs, and of the same body and partakers of his promise in Christ by the gospel.*" Therefore, Ephesians doesn't teach that God predestines elect individuals to irresistible salvation by limited atonement, to the exclusion of all remaining individuals who are not pre-chosen. Ephesians and the rest of the Bible teaches that in Jesus Christ, all who trust in Christ, both Jew and Gentile, will receive redemption, (**Rom. 9:24-26; 10:12-13; 11:25-26**). "*But when the fullness of time was come, God sent forth his son… To redeem them that were under the law* (Israel), *that we* (Gentiles) *might receive the adoption of sons* (**Gal. 4:4-5**).

The truth of man's responsibility to exercise his faith is taught in many places of Scripture! Consider Jesus' parable of the 'Talents' (**Matthew 25:14-30**). Jesus rejected the faithless servant who had received one talent, calling him wicked, slothful, and unprofitable! Consider again the parable of the 'Sower and Soils' that we reviewed in the context of spiritual-warfare in Chapter 3. Jesus explains this parable in all three Gospels (**Matthew 13, Mark 4,** and **Luke 8**), identifying the sower's 'seed' as God's Word being proclaimed by the preacher. Notice that God didn't send impotent seed to bad ground, and efficacious seed to the good ground! Every seed of the Word is capable of producing fruit and never returns void (**Isaiah 55:11**)! It returns producing either "*goodness*" or "*severity*" (**Romans 11:22-23**). The 'ground' the Seed falls on determines whether it will germinate unto life. Consider also the 'Rich Young Ruler' (**Mark 10:17-22**), who humbly and excitedly ran to Jesus seeking the inheritance of eternal life. Jesus loved him, and personally and directly offered for him to surrender all and follow Him as His disciple. Yet, the young man departed sadly because he was unwilling to risk losing his possessions in order to receive what Jesus had offered him. Jesus never offers anything He's unwilling to give! But the person to whom eternal life is offered, must willfully and repentantly receive it by faith (**James 1:21**)! Let's not forget King Agrippa (**Acts 26:27-29**). In response to Paul's preaching Christ in the relaying of his testimony to Agrippa, he (Agrippa) confessed he was 'almost persuaded' to be a Christian. Paul passionately answered, expressing his hope that he (Agrippa) and all hearing him (Paul) would be not "*almost*," but "*altogether*" persuaded to believe!

Every aspect of salvation is procured by God with no element of contribution from man. Even the faith to receive is provided by God (**Romans 12:3**)! Yet man must believe God and by faith receive his salvation. Stretching out a hand, by an undeserving person who by faith believes that what is being offered can be his if he just receives it, is not a work that contributes to his gift! So is salvation *received*. It is the simple exercise of believing faith that God demands from us (**Hebrews 11:6**). Our holy God who "*cannot lie*" (**Titus 1:2**), nor "*tempteth He any man*" (**James 1:13**), will never offer something that He has no intention of giving. Will He speak and "*not make it good?*" (**Numbers 23:19**).

The result of these rigid misinterpretations of Scripture related to salvation greatly affect the life of the Church! Calvinistic churches reject the practice of 'altar calls' and the utilization of 'sinner's prayers' in leading new believers to Christ. They're strong on their doctrinal teachings but tend to remain impassionate on evangelistic efforts because of their beliefs concerning God's sovereign predestination program. They may go through some motions of evangelism, thinking that God can use those avenues as a means to bring His elect people in, but there's generally no fire behind those efforts. On the opposite end of the spectrum, many fervent Baptist ministries tend to over-emphasize their efforts on 'soul-winning,' viewing it as their sole reason for existence and generally make it their church's number one 'Great Commission' priority. There is always a salvation message in their preaching, followed by an altar-call with pleadings, coupled with well-meaning shaming, guilt and pressure tactics as a means to urge people to respond. The inevitable lack of response from use of these tactics often leads to frustration and the introduction of more people-drawing gimmicks. Believers in these services may often feel beat down as not meeting expectations of productivity if they don't at every opportunity invite new unsaved acquaintances in. Their zeal for soul-winning is fueled by obligation, almost as if their approval by God and their salvation depended on it. Pentecostals may be somewhere in between those extremes, but like the Corinthian Church, if the manifestational gifts are in operation without Biblical decency and order, visitors may recoil and justly write them off as 'kooks' (**1 Corinthians 14:23**).

With regards to the 'preservation of the saints,' those who embrace the doctrine of eternal security agree that God does not make bad 'investments.' Because we're shortsighted, we may invest in the stock market and the value of our investment may decrease, or potentially even be completely lost. But because God is omniscient, knowing the end from the beginning, and perfect in all his works, he doesn't pick bad "stocks" that result in bankruptcy. If God, foreknowing all our good and bad free-will choices, invests His Spirit in us for regeneration, it is inconceivable that the genuinely converted person should turn out to surprise God by falling away again into perdition! That eventuality would render God incapable of foreknowing and keeping his own children safe from perditional harm. It would be in direct violation of the promise of **Jude 24**, which states, "*Now unto him that is able to keep you from falling, and to present you faultless before the presence of his glory with exceeding joy.*" It would render void Jesus' assurance of **John 10:28** which states, "*I give unto them eternal life; and they shall never perish, neither shall any man pluck them out of my hand.*"

Having said that, the Arminian might argue it's possible that God, for his own sovereign and eternal purposes, may do just that (*reject someone He's redeemed*) for a reason presently unknown and incomprehensible to us. Some possible examples may be: Judas Iscariot who was hand picked by Jesus himself; Simon the Sorcerer who like the others believed the Gospel and was baptized (**Acts 8:13**); Demas who forsook Paul because he loved this present world (**2 Timothy 4:10**); or prideful Diotrephes who is condemned by the Apostle John (**3 John 11**). Also, in the book of Revelation, Jesus warns the Ephesian church to repent, or risk their candlestick being removed from its place (**Revelation 2:5**). And, in Jesus' warning to the Church at Sardis, the possibility is implied for those who fail to be overcomers that their names could be blotted out from the Book of Life (**Revelation 3:5**).

It may very well be that some of the above individuals, and others like them not mentioned here, were either never genuinely regenerated, or that perhaps they eventually corrected their ways as they heeded correction and matured further in their walk with Christ. Although God doesn't use false threats to correct His children, this is generally the Calvinistic view. But the Arminian would argue that these were indeed in genuine relationship with Christ, but that they turned away from him, back "*to the weak and beggarly elements... of ...bondage,*" (**Galatians 4:9**). Arminians recoil at what they term as "cheap grace," where a saved person who continues a sinful lifestyle, does so without any substantial eternal consequence.

But, the strongest of the "Arminian" arguments noted above against eternal security can be adequately answered: Judas Iscariot was always an anti-Christ-type "son of perdition" (**John 17:12; 2 Thessalonians 2:3**); Likewise Simon 'the Sorcerer' was an imposter (**Acts 8:21**), as Jesus and the Apostles have warned us (**Matthew 7:15; 2 Peter 2:1; 1 John 4:1**); The Ephesian church was warned of forfeiting their "candlestick" (*place of usefulness and service to God*), not their salvation; Regarding Sardis' warning – at the end there are several books opened (**Revelation 20:12**), not just one. The Lamb's Book of Life (*book of the 'righteous'*) is not the same as the "book of life" (i.e., *book of the 'living'*), which Scripture suggests is a registry with details of all those born and alive at any point in time on the earth (**Psalms 69:28; 87:6; 139:16**). God can bring chastisement to those He loves, and even 'prematurely terminate' a human life on earth without 'eternally killing' his spirit into perdition (**Psalms 94:10-14; 1 Cor. 11:30; Hebrews 12:6**).

In the context of this discussion, some may also suggest that we can't always keep a sovereign, omnipotent, and omniscient God in a narrow box of "black and whites," as we're able to see them. One could argue that for His greater purposes, some of which we can now understand, God has at times appeared to contradict his own rules and stated expectations, and has led some of his people to do what would otherwise be clearly condemned by Him. Some examples might be when God chose the younger over the elder (**Genesis 25:23; Romans 9:12**), or when He instructed Abraham to commit human sacrifice (**Genesis 22:2**), or when He instructed his minister Hosea to marry a prostitute (**Hosea 1:2; Leviticus 21:7,13-14**). While we can now look back and understand why God did what he did, at the time the instructions were given God's servants had to be unmistakably convinced that they weren't misreading Him. God's rules never changed, but He specifically led these individuals to temporarily act in apparent contradiction to those rules, for a purpose. Nevertheless, God made provision, and at no time is there a hint in Scripture that any of these were in danger of placing their eternal salvation in peril.

To be fair, it must also be brought out that the Bible does warn believers not to backslide. For example, those who have begun their walk with Christ are cautioned not to violate their liberty in the new Christian Covenant by returning to the bondage of Old Testament Law (**Galatians 5:1**). In Christ, the ceremonial Law of sacrifices was fulfilled, made obsolete, and rendered of non-effect. Paul's admonishments capsulated in **Hebrews 6:4-6** and **Galatians 5:4** speak to this. Those who remained persistent in returning to a finished law system risked the consequences of unbelief, preferring to trust in an obsolete system over God's provision of Christ for their salvation. Additionally, in this discussion of the possibility for regenerated man to fall away, the proponents of this view will cite the Bible where it speaks of a 'latter-day apostasy.' In **2 Thessalonians 2:3**[8] the term "falling away" comes from the Greek word *apostasia*[9], which Strong defines as, "defection from truth, falling away, *to* forsake."

Biblical analysis affirms that the reborn spirit cannot fall away. Backsliding is an act of the <u>soul</u>, not the spirit. In large part, it matters much how healthy and disciplined our soul is because it directly affects the freedom or oppression of our spirit. A vexed soul can weigh down one's spirit, but it can't cause it to die. The Apostle Paul told the Corinthians, "*We are troubled on every side, yet not distressed; we are perplexed, but not in despair; Persecuted, but not forsaken; cast down, but not destroyed,*" (**2 Corinthians 4:8-9**). It is safe for us to believe God fully when His Word says that, "*The gifts and calling of God are without repentance*" (**Romans 11:29**). God doesn't make mistakes. He isn't surprised by our failures and He doesn't change his mind. God doesn't have mood swings causing us to fall out of favor with him because we may have in some way disappointed him. God's Word and his loving mercy endures forever (**Psalm 136**; **1 Peter 1:23-25**). Our hope in Him is sure and steadfast, "*as an anchor of the soul*" (**Hebrews 6:19**). God's promise is, "*I will never leave thee, nor forsake thee*" (**Hebrews 13:5**).

When God by his Spirit causes a sinner to be born-again, he is 'passed from death unto life.' Jesus used this expression in his response to critics after healing the impotent man on the Sabbath. He said, "*Verily, verily, I say unto you, He that heareth my word, and believeth on him that sent me, hath everlasting life, and shall not come into condemnation; but is passed from death unto life,*" (**John 5:24**). There is no room in the sampling of verses cited in this chapter for the possibility of any outcome other than what's clearly stated: Salvation is initiated, effected, and sustained by God, and the believer is therefore secure.

The rebirth of our spirit by God is real, it is safe, and it cannot be lost. However, in our souls we are repeatedly admonished to be faithful! Esau sold his birthright (**Genesis 25:33**). He didn't lose it, and no one took it from him. At that moment of vulnerability, he valued it less than the temporal satisfaction of a carnal appetite. As a result, in the epistle to the **Hebrews** (**12:16**), Esau was equated as a 'fornicator' and a 'profane person,' and his action was irreversible. Though Esau did permanently lose his rightful first-born position of honor, he didn't cease being a son of Isaac. Similarly, the repentant "prodigal son" was received back with all the honors of 'sonship,' but his spent inheritance was now forfeited and not restored. The prodigal's elder brother was now heir to all that remained (**Luke 15:31**). The prodigal lost the rewards of his inheritance, but not his relationship.

We're comforted in knowing that once God, by his foreknowledge, accepts us and grants us eternal life by causing the regeneration of our spirits, we are "*always confident*" that His Spirit within us is the "*earnest*," or 'down payment,' of our eternal salvation (**2 Corinthians 5:5-6**). While with God's enabling we're called to safeguard the blessings of this precious and incomparable gift, there is no safer place in the universe to be, than "in Christ." Thiessen stated it succinctly, "Union with Christ means eternal security."[10]

B. Sanctification of Man's Soul

At the moment of regeneration of man's spirit, an immediate conflict is born. It is a tug-of-war between the Spirit of God now residing within us, and our carnal flesh. The Apostle Paul put it this way: "*For the flesh lusteth against the Spirit, and the Spirit against the flesh: and these are contrary the one to the other: so that ye cannot do the things that ye would*," (**Galatians 5:17**). God's Spirit quickens our human spirit and becomes one with it. Therefore, the battlefield for this conflict between the re-born spirit and the flesh, is the <u>soul</u>. *Positional* sanctification declares that we have been set apart unto a holy God, and that our ultimate destiny is to spend eternity with him in perfection.

As discussed earlier, man's three-dimensional soul is his intellect, emotions, and will. Man's soul is greatly affected by the Spirit of God. When God convicts us of sin, we understand it with our minds, we feel the sorrow and regret of it with our emotions, and by exercising our free will we're able to decide what to do about it. Intellectual and emotional joy, peace, and hope results by yielding to the Spirit of God. Similarly, man's soul is also greatly affected by our carnal flesh. Regardless of the total transformation in the renewed spirit of man that results from regeneration, his body remains vulnerable to carnality, greed, corruption, and cravings of lusts. Upon being born again, John reminds us that, "*It is the spirit that quickeneth; the flesh profiteth nothing*," (**John 6:63a**). Our carnality is still mortal and it pulls on the mind to entertain harmful thoughts, causing our emotions to crave the fleshly appetites, leaving our will with the great burden of decision as to whether we're going to yield to the desire, or dismiss it by ignoring and fleeing the temptation. Satan capitalizes on the weaknesses of the flesh, and if allowed entry will exert much pressure on the soul to capitulate to his temptations.

Therefore, to will to do right, the soul requires discipline and fortification. Overcoming the flesh by strengthening the intellect, emotions and will, produces *progressive* sanctification for the soul. It is obvious that just because one's spirit is regenerated, it doesn't mean the individual can't again fall into temptation and sin. Strengthening the inner man doesn't happen automatically, it is a life-long endeavor. The soul can be strengthened by human effort and by divine intervention. God provides the power, but to get it, the believer's efforts of yielding his will in obedience to God is required. Human effort involves the discipline to pray, to study God's Word, to join with a local body of believers, and to live accordingly. Divine help is derived from these activities of discipline, but it is also received from yielding to the available supernatural infusion of power by the Holy Spirit.

Consider this: God promises He will liberally give wisdom to those who ask Him for it (**James 1:5**). But if wisdom is the proper application of knowledge, then *knowledge* is the needed ingredient for wisdom to operate! God doesn't promise to give us knowledge. Rather, He exhorts us to willfully pursue and obtain it (numerous passages in **Proverbs**, such as... **1:5, 2:1-7, 9:10, 10:14, 14:6, 18:15**). Once we've been diligent to obtain the knowledge of God, He will grant us the wisdom to apply it. Simply stated, the gist of what God is saying to us is; 'pursue and acquire knowledge – along the way come to Me so that I may liberally bless you with the wisdom for how to apply that gained knowledge.'

Sanctification of the soul is a progressive occurrence in the life of the believer. It also is a three-dimensional process. We are *positionally* sanctified at the moment of regeneration. When the Apostle Paul writes his corrective epistle to the Corinthian church (**1 Corinthians 3:1, 6:11**), he confirms that they are already declared "*sanctified*" (**1 Corinthians 1:2**)[11] We are also *progressively* being sanctified as we grow in faith and our Christian maturity. When he writes to the **Romans** (**12:2**)[12], the Apostle Paul admonishes his readers to not be conformed to this world, but to rather be transformed in their minds (the key element of man's soul). Finally, at the return of Christ we will be ultimately, completely, and *permanently* sanctified upon our translation into the glorified state. **Hebrews 10:14** speaks of our eternal "perfection"[13] as being the end result of Christ's offering.

C. Glorification of Man's Body

The epistle to the Romans is perhaps the most theologically profound of Paul's inspired writings. Placed immediately after the four Gospels and Acts, it stands as a posted introductory 'sentinel' to the rest of the New Testament Epistles that follow it. In **Romans**, the Apostle deals with three major lifetime themes: *Condemnation* (**1:18-3:20**), *Justification* (**3:21-5:21**), and *Sanctification* (**6:1-7:25**). He adds one afterlife theme: *Glorification* (**8:1-39**). After establishing our condemnation because of sin, Paul deals with the remaining three campaigns of God to accomplish our final salvation. In the soteriological progression, after justification and sanctification, glorification is the third and final outcome of the transformational process.

Justification is the declaration of God that in Christ we have been made righteous. It is positional, and the result of regeneration of our spirits. God then sets us apart as a result of the redemption process, unto *sanctification*. Romans deals primarily with the discipline and maturation of the soul that separates us from the world. It is an exhortation to flee sin and to pursue obedience to God, and the righteousness He has called us to. *Glorification* is the end result, which will not be achieved until our mortal bodies are made immortal by a direct act of God resulting from the "*first resurrection*" (**Revelation 20:6**).

A person may experience genuine salvation and bring forth the spiritual fruit that results from a regenerated spirit, but as we have already discussed, his soul continues to struggle with the temptations of his thought life. His inner spirit is willing is to do right, while his carnal passions relentlessly pull him to do wrong. Furthermore, even though a believer may experience the glorious divine physical healing of a diseased body, that restored body housing the regenerated spirit remains virtually unchanged, in the sense that it is just as mortal, carnal, and fleshly as it was before the healing or conversion. That physical mortal state of vulnerability continues until the ultimate moment of time when God completes his redemption process by glorifying man's corporal body. That glorification occurs at the return of Christ, when the dead in Christ are resurrected and those who are alive at the time of his coming are raptured (**1 Thessalonians 4:16-17**[14]). In his epistle to the

Romans (8:11), Paul put it this way, "*But if the Spirit of him that raised up Jesus from the dead dwell in you, he that raised up Christ from the dead shall also quicken your mortal bodies by his Spirit that dwelleth in you.*"

The conclusion of this chapter is that, as a trichotomy, man's salvation is accomplished by God in three integrated but successive stages. The initial phase of regeneration of the spirit sets forth the course of the progression. Once the human spirit has been made alive by the Spirit of God, there is no Biblical support for the belief that the spirit can be subsequently abandoned by God unto death. However, the soul requires the application of faith and discipline to stay spiritually healthy. The soul can mature and thrive in one's walk with Christ, or it can grow cold, distant, and fruitless. One's desire to serve God and yield to his promises can open the heavenly windows of God's supernatural blessings upon the soul for spiritual enrichment and enhanced enablement, to include the operation of spiritual gifts. Neglecting to build up the soul through conventional means (i.e., Christian fellowship, church assembly, Bible study and prayer), and supernatural means (the Spirit's giftings), can render a person unable to reach his full spiritual potential. Neglecting the soul disciplines renders us spiritually weakened and vulnerable to the wiles of Satan. A person can so starve his soul, or be lured and entangled again in a sin-prone lifestyle, to result in finding himself in a backslidden condition. Backsliding can spiral downwards to such a critical level as to render the person feeling he is unable to repent and restore his fellowship with God. But God is faithful! There is no conclusive Scriptural evidence to determine that even at this low condition a regenerated person's spirit can again be rendered dead (unsaved). The Apostle Paul deals with this extreme condition in his epistles:

"*If any man's work shall be burned, he shall suffer loss: but he himself shall be saved; yet so as by fire,*" (**1 Corinthians 3:15**);

"*To deliver such an one to Satan for the destruction of the flesh, that the spirit may be saved in the day of the Lord Jesus,*" (**1 Corinthians 5:5**);

"*Of whom is Hymenaeus and Alexander; whom I have delivered unto Satan, that they may learn not to blaspheme,*" (**1 Timothy 1:20**).

We can therefore agree that God desires our spirit, soul, and body to be sanctified and preserved blameless in honor and expectation of His coming (**1 Thessalonians 5:23**). However, varying theological perspectives affect our understanding of this truth. With regard to Calvinism versus Arminianism; the Reformed Christian is the staunch '5-Point' Calvinist, while evangelical Baptists may at best be '2-Pointers.' The Baptist will accept 'Total Depravity' in a modified manner that leaves the unbeliever with a faith capability component that he's responsible for, he'll reject 'Unconditional Election' (i.e., *predestination*), 'Limited Atonement' in its purest Reformed sense, and 'Irresistible Grace,' but will embrace "Eternal Security' (*"Perseverance of the saints"*). Many Pentecostals, as well as Methodists and the like, are more closely aligned to Arminianism, and are perhaps only '1-Pointers.' With similar views as the Baptist concerning the first four Calvinistic "T.U.L.I.P.," points, they will likely add Eternal Security for the unfaithful in the rejection column.

But better comprehension through the tri-fold operations of God, attempted to be laid out throughout the chapters of this *Soul Baptism* book, will hopefully help alleviate the seemingly impassable obstacles for a more unified understanding and cooperative fellowship between Christian brethren.

CHAPTER FIVE ENDNOTES

[1] J.D. Douglas and Philip W. Comfort, eds., *Who's Who in Christian History*, (Wheaton: Tyndale House, 1992), 128.

[2] Herbert Lockyer, *All the Doctrines of the Bible*, (Grand Rapids: Zondervan, 1964), 223.

[3] Enns, 463.

[4] Douglas, 36.

[5] Enns, 489.

[6] Lockyer, 223.

[7] Enns, 489.

[8] *"Let no man deceive you by any means, for that day shall not come, except there come a falling away first, and that man of sin be revealed, the son of perdition,"* (**2 Thessalonians 2:3**).

[9] Strong's Greek Dictionary of the New Testament, Word #646.

[10] Thiessen, 284.

[11] *"And such were some of you: but ye are washed, but ye are sanctified, but ye are justified in the name of the Lord Jesus, and by the Spirit of our God,"* (**1 Corinthians 6:11**).

[12] *"And be not conformed to this world: but be ye transformed by the renewing of your mind, that ye may prove what is that good, and acceptable, and perfect, will of God,"* (**Romans 12:2**).

[13] *"For by one offering he hath perfected for ever them that are sanctified,"* (**Hebrews 10:14**).

[14] *"For the Lord himself shall descend from heaven with a shout, with the voice of the archangel, and with the trump of God: and the dead in Christ shall rise first: Then we which are alive and remain shall be caught up together with them in the clouds, to meet the Lord in the air: and so shall we ever be with the Lord,"* (**1 Thessalonians 4:16-17**).

CHAPTER 6
THE THREE-FOLD ASPECT OF SALVATION

"Even when we were dead in sins,
[God] hath <u>quickened</u> us together with Christ, (by grace ye are
saved;) And hath <u>raised</u> us up together, and made us <u>sit</u> together in
heavenly places in Christ Jesus:"
Ephesians 2:5-6

We've already touched on the idea that God accomplishes our salvation in three phases: positionally, progressively, and permanently. The above verses lay out this progression of salvation. First we are *"quickened"* by the Spirit so that we are *positioned* in right relationship with God the Father. Then we are *"raised up,"* during our Christian lifetime, *sanctified* as we walk with Him, as well as up to the time of our resurrection, so that we are progressively drawn closer to Him. Finally we are made to *"sit together"* with Christ in heavenly places, where, in our *glorified* state, we will rule and reign with Him for ever. Note that each phase is "together with," and because of, Christ.

In **Romans 8:29-30**, the Apostle Paul explains that those who God quickens and will ultimately glorify, are those he 'foreknew' (i.e., God knowing men's hearts, and how they will exercise their free-will faith in response to His drawing them to salvation): *"For whom he did foreknow, he also did predestinate to be conformed to the image of his Son, that he might be the firstborn among many brethren. Moreover whom he* *did predestinate, them he also called: and whom he called, them he also justified: and whom he justified, them he also glorified."*

Therefore, the three-fold aspect of salvation for believers is sovereignly decreed based on God's foreknowledge, and it unfolds in the three phases we call; *positional, progressive,* and *permanent* salvation. In this chapter we'll look at salvation from the perspective of these three phases.

A. Positional Salvation

When we declare that we are *positionally* saved, it means that in God's eyes we have been placed in right standing with Him, we have been positioned by Him to identify with his sheep and not the goats (**Matthew 25:32-33**[1]), and we have been brought into a 'sonship' relationship with Him. As sons of God we have been made, *"heirs of God, and joint-heirs with Christ"* (**Romans 8:17a**).

Understanding our positional salvation is based on such biblical passages as the Apostle John's proclamation in his First Epistle (**1 John 5:13a**), *"These things have I written unto you that believe on the name of the Son of God; that ye may know that ye have eternal life."* This passage declares that, by faith in God's promise, we are assured that we already possess our eternal salvation. It terms our salvation in the past tense, affirming we who have believed as having ownership in the promise of an already completed feat. There is no suggestion for the possibility that it still remains an unfinished work. The work of salvation is completed, but we have yet to experience the full possession of that glorified state of salvation that has already been officially and irreversibly assigned to us.

We must all concede that after having been converted and regenerated, we continue to struggle with sin in this life, and that we don't at the moment of salvation become sinless or physically enter the heavenlies. It must therefore be understood that positional salvation is based in the fact that our *spirits* have been "quickened," or regenerated. Regeneration is a finished product that is complete and permanent, not requiring any additional divine work. It is, however, a foundational work that for now is limited to our spirits. It will, but has not yet, completely affected our souls and bodies.

The Apostle Paul, writing to the **Philippians (1:6)**, speaks to this truth in terms of hope and assurance when he says, *"Being confident of this very thing, that he which hath begun a good work in you will perform it until the day of Jesus Christ."* Paul is referring to our spirits' renewal as being the first phase of our eventual total salvation. He is approaching the subject with full confidence that if God has invested His Spirit in us, He will carry the rest through to completion. The 'rest' He's referring to is our souls, and ultimately even our bodies. The *"day of Jesus Christ"* is in reference to his Second Coming at the end of the age, when the total salvation of our tri-part beings is finally completed.

B. Progressive Salvation

Progressive salvation has nothing whatsoever to do with perfecting ourselves or earning favor with God through our performance efforts of good works. Rather, it is a God-ordained discipleship process of being *"conformed to the image of his Son,"* (**Romans 8:29-30**). It is a maturing and growing relationship with God of progressive renewal, resulting from what He initiated in us. It is the time for our spiritual fruitfulness (**Matthew 7:16; Galatians 5:22-24**). As this chapter's Scripture text suggests, God is *"raising us up"* together with Christ.

Similar to a healthy relationship with a spouse, one becomes more familiar, comfortable, intimate, appreciative, and compatible with his life partner as the years together progress. So too, in our progressive relationship with God. We learn to trust and rely on him more and more as our walk of faith is seasoned with deepening experience. We become more like Him. Not in the sense that we, in this earthly body, develop divine attributes, but in that we begin to think more like God as we live out our lives and are less surprised or disturbed by life's mishaps. This growing relationship is nurtured by communing with God through prayer and by nourishing ourselves with his Word. This process of communion is further helped through the regular fellowship and assembling together of the saints in church-related settings. There is no possibility for securing our relationship with God by pleasing him through the performance of 'good works.' Because we are still sinful beings, our 'righteous' works are as the 'fruit of a poisonous tree.' God calls *"all our righteousnesses...as filthy rags"* (**Isaiah 64:6**). Our salvation is totally unmerited in every phase. Believing faith is what pleases God

(**Hebrews 11:6**). God was well-pleased with His Son before Jesus had accomplished any work at all (**Matthew 3:17**)! Our progressive salvation is all by God's grace, because it is by His provision that we are even enabled the opportunity to commune with Him.

It is evident therefore, that progressive salvation is has to do with the sanctification of man's *soul*. It deals with the spiritual maturing of man's intellect, emotions and will. We discussed it in chapter 5-B as *sanctification* of the soul. Progressive salvation is the molding of our souls which is conducted by God, but requires the willing cooperation of man. Throughout our earthly lives, God's desire is to transform us into the image of his Son. But because we retain our free will, we must be willing to be molded. Resisting this process results in an incomplete, immature creature that has missed its opportunity for full usefulness and reward potential. Our reluctance comes from the enjoyment of carnal imperfections. God can foresee what he wants to make us into. God's aim is ultimate perfection which He will achieve. We cannot see, nor fully conceive, the final product. Our carnal nature is comfortable with the sin we enjoy, and even the godliest of us is reluctant to and incapable of complete abstinence from it. Though we may comprehend enough truth to recognize we ought to abstain from even the appearance of evil and let God have full reign over our lives, we cannot, except through incremental steps, with God's help, work towards mortifying our carnal nature. In and of ourselves, we are completely helpless. Without God's help we cannot achieve progressive salvation. But in Christ's strength we can do all things (**Philippians 4:13**)!

In *Mere Christianity*, CS Lewis discusses this life-long struggle between the determination of God to ultimately perfect us, and our reluctance for God to accomplish this in us because of our sin and sense of self-sufficiency:

> "…we must never imagine that our own unaided efforts can be relied on to carry us even through the next twenty-four hours as 'decent' people. If He does not support us, not one of us is safe from some gross sin. On the other hand, no possible degree of holiness or heroism which has ever been recorded of the greatest of saints is beyond what He is determined to produce in every one of us in the end. The job will not be

completed in this life; but He means to get us as far as possible before death."[2]

When a saved individual falls into sin, his permanent *salvation* isn't forfeited, but rather, his progressive *sanctification* is hindered. It is Satan who lays his snares for us to sin. It is in these vulnerable times of weakness that Satan does his best to do us as much damage as possible through condemnation that often results in self-isolation. Instead of condemnation, God brings conviction, which if heeded leads us to repentance and forgiveness that restores the joy of salvation. Jesus Christ is our interceding advocate in these matters (**Romans 8:34; Hebrews 7:25; 1 John 2:1**).

B. Permanent Salvation

Some have attempted to achieve human soul-perfection either through a system of works or a state of mind. Ascetics believe they can achieve a state of perfection before God through a life of rigorous religious self-denial. At the other end of the spectrum, I have personally known some 'ultra' Calvinists, who ignoring such basic Biblical content as the "Lord's Prayer" (**Matthew 6:9-13; Luke 11:2-4**), or **1 John 1:8-10**,[3] believed that at the moment of salvation all of their sins, past, present and future, were blotted out in such a way that even acknowledging a wrong or asking for forgiveness for a failure in a post-conversion prayer amounts to a superfluous lack of faith that's an offensive insult to God. In both cases, either through human effort, or through mental 'hyper-faith,' these two groups of believers seem to think they have reached a sufficient God-pleasing level of perfection.

But, being made to *sit* together with Christ refers to a future and final aspect of our salvation when we will actually, and in reality, dwell and reign forever in His very presence! At that time, and not before then, we will achieve our perfected state. We will have to be in our perfected and glorified state at that time because our holy God cannot have sin dwell in His presence. God is a consuming fire (**Deuteronomy 4:24**). Saved or not, in this life we are sinful beings. We are warned that no man, because of his sin, can see God and live (**Exodus 33:20**). Yet, we are promised that we shall see him as He is, face to face (**1 John 3:2**). There is no contradiction here. In this carnal state we cannot ever see God to a full extent and survive with our lives intact. But in our glorified state, when we will be in our sinless perfection, we will be able to interact with God face to face because, *"we shall be like him; for we shall see Him as He is"* (**1 John 3:2**). There are numerous Scripture passages that deal with this truth: **1 Corinthians 15:52-54**; **Philippians 3:21**; and, are a couple more examples.[4]

Therefore, *permanent* salvation is the final phase of the Christian's 'blessed hope' that is fulfilled by his rapture/resurrection at the Second Coming of Christ. The editors of the work entitled, *A Guide to Biblical Prophecy*, state it this way:

> "…the return of Jesus Christ will mean the full experience of salvation for the people of God. The biblical emphasis is on the resurrection of the body (1 Corinthians 15) at the return of Christ rather than on the salvation of the soul in conversion or at death, though orthodox theology rightly emphasizes union with Christ both in conversion and at death. But although we have experienced a foretaste of salvation in the present and look forward to being 'with Christ' when we die (unless Christ comes first), we also can be assured that we will be resurrected at His coming. Because Christ has been raised from the dead, those who belong to Christ also can confidently expect to be resurrected at the *parousia* (**1 Corinthians 15:20-23**)."[5]

Therefore, our salvation unfolds brilliantly. Our spirits are quickened so that we become *positionally* saved. Our souls, by God's grace, as evidenced by our fruitful works, are *progressively* being saved through sanctification. Lastly, our carnal bodies will be resurrected and changed into perfected temples, which will allow us to *permanently* enjoy the full experience and benefits of our glorified salvation in the very presence of God! We will rule and reign with Him as *"heirs of God, and joint-heirs with Christ"* (**Romans 8:17**). As we can begin to see more clearly, understanding this progression of salvation from the three-dimensional perspective of spirit, soul, and body, harmonizes many of the divisive and opposing positions held by those who identify themselves with Arminian and Calvinist theology.

CHAPTER SIX ENDNOTES

[1] *"And before him shall be gathered all nations: and he shall separate them one from another, as a shepherd divideth his sheep from the goats: And he shall set the sheep on his right hand, but the goats on the left,"* (**Matthew 25:32-33**).

[2] CS Lewis, *Mere Christianity*, (San Francisco: Harper Collins Publishers, 1952), 204.

[3] *"If we say that we have no sin, we deceive ourselves, and the truth is not in us. If we confess our sins, he is faithful and just to forgive us our sins, and to cleanse us from all unrighteousness. If we say that we have not sinned, we make him a liar, and his word is not in us,"* (**1 John 1:8-10**).

[4] *"In a moment, in the twinkling of an eye, at the last trump: for the trumpet shall sound, and the dead shall be raised incorruptible, and we shall be changed. For this corruptible must put on incorruption, and this mortal must put on immortality. So when this corruptible shall have put on incorruption, and this mortal shall have put on immortality, then shall be brought to pass the saying that is written, Death is swallowed up in victory,"* (**1 Corinthians 15:52-54**); (*Jesus Christ*) *...Who shall change our vile body, that it may be fashioned like unto his glorious body, according to the working whereby he is able even to subdue all things unto himself,"* (**Philippians 3:21**); *Beloved, now are we the sons of God, and it doth not yet appear what we shall be: but we know that, when he shall appear, we shall be like him; for we shall see him as he is,* (**1 John 3:2**).

[5] Carl E. Armstrong and W. Ward Gasque, ed., *A Guide to Biblical Prophecy*, (Peabody, MA: Hendrickson Publishers, 1989), 246-247.

SECTION THREE:

GOD, MAN, AND PROVISION FOR EMPOWERMENT

CHAPTER 7
THE THREE OFFICES OF CHRIST

"And Joshua said, Alas, O <u>Lord GOD</u>, wherefore hast thou at all brought this people over Jordan, to deliver us into the hand of the Amorites, to destroy us? would to <u>God</u> we had been content, and dwelt on the other side Jordan!"
Joshua 7:7

The above verse may seem a curious choice for this topic. However, it is to my knowledge the only verse in the Bible that contains all three elements of the point to be made in this chapter.

There are many names used to describe God in the Bible. But in theology there are three primary names for God. They are: Jehovah, Elohim, and Adonai. The King James Bible translators were very careful to distinguish these three primary names in their English translation. Therefore, whenever the original ***Jehovah*** appears, they translated it as "GOD" or "LORD," always with all letters in the uppercase. ***Elohim*** is always translated as "God" or "god(s)," with the first letter "G" capitalized if the reference is to the true God. The word 'god(s)' in all lowercase letters refers to other 'deities' of human invention. ***Adonai*** is always translated as "Lord." Only the first letter "L" is capitalized. **Joshua 7:7** contains all three primary names of God in the same verse.

In Judeo-Christian theology there are also three primary offices found in the Bible. They are: **Prophet**, **Priest**, and **King**. Initiation into each of these offices required a ceremonial unction with oil, symbolic of the Holy Spirit's identification and empowerment for service to the particular office. No one was allowed to hold more than one office. Jesus Christ is the only individual in the Bible to be officially anointed to occupy all three of these offices.

Some Bible figures functioned in the roles of one or more of these three offices, but none other than Jesus possessed the appointed authority of the offices. For example, Moses acted as a prophet in bringing God's laws to man. He acted as a priest when he continually interceded for the Israelites before God. He also functioned as a king as he protectively led God's people out of Egyptian bondage towards the Promised Land. However, Moses was never officially ordained by an anointing with oil into any of these offices. Jesus however, at his baptism by John the Baptist, received the highest possible anointing for the offices he was to hold. When Jesus was baptized, he wasn't merely identified as God's choice by men. At Jesus' baptism, God's own voice from heaven identified Him as the Christ. Neither did Jesus receive a symbolic anointing with oil administered by another man. God the Holy Spirit came Himself from heaven upon Jesus to anoint and empower him!

What I am suggesting in the introduction to this chapter that deals with the three offices of Christ, is that the three primary names for God correlate with the three offices of Christ. The three offices of Christ provide for us all we need to secure our salvation.

A. Christ the Prophet

A prophet is God's spokesperson who speaks to man the words of God. Of the three primary names for God, *Jehovah* stands out as the most supreme. In quoting Moses Maimonides, the Jewish commentator of the Middle Ages, Nathan Stone in his book, *Names of God*, writes:

> "All the names of God which occur in Scripture are derived from His works except one, and that is Jehovah; and this is called the plain name, because it teaches plainly and unequivocally of the substance of God … The Hebrew may say *the* Elohim, the true God, in opposition to all false gods; but he never says *the* Jehovah, for Jehovah is the name of the true God only. He says again and again, my God or my Elohim, but never my *Jehovah*,

for when he says my God he means Jehovah. He speaks of the God (*Elohim*) *of Israel* but never *the Jehovah of Israel,* for there is no other Jehovah."[1]

Therefore, God's supreme name ***Jehovah*** alludes to Christ as the **Prophet** who through the hypostatic union, in the ultimate manner, reveals God to man. Jesus Christ is, without dispute, the incomparable Prophet! Both the Old and New Testaments are filled with references to the Messiah as the supreme Prophet.

The first chapter of the Apostle John's Gospel (**John 1:19-28**) records for us that Jesus' forerunner, John the Baptist, was interrogated by a delegation of priests and Levites, sent by the chief Pharisees at Jerusalem into the wilderness where John was preaching. They asked him three questions: If he was the Christ; if he was Elias; and if he was "*that Prophet*"? Jewish theology in those days incorrectly interpreted the "Prophet" mentioned in **Deuteronomy 18:15**[2] as a third individual apart from the coming Messiah, or Elias, who Malachi at the very end of the Old Testament (**Malachi 4:5**[3]), said would be sent before the 'Day of the Lord.' John the Baptist denied being the Christ, Elias, nor "that (*incorrect*) Prophet." Both Peter and Stephen, as later recorded in the book of **Acts** (**3:22** and **7:37**), clarified that "that (*true*) Prophet" was none other than Jesus Christ.

After triumphantly resisting the Devil and putting him to flight by rebuffing his wilderness temptations, Jesus begins to preach his message, declaring, as recorded in the Gospels; "*Repent: for the kingdom of heaven is at hand*" (**Matthew 4:17b**). As the ultimate Prophet of God, Jesus appeared on the earth's scene with the Father's Gospel message of good news. Jesus said he was bringing to man the very *words* of God (**John 5:19-47** and **14:10**)! Because as the perfect Prophet, "*...being the brightness of his glory, and the express image of his person*" (**Hebrews 1:3a**), Jesus was the very manifestation of God the Father. As the perfect divine revelation, Jesus the **Prophet**, is fully authoritative in providing for us perfect **positional** salvation.

B. Christ the Priest

A priest functions as man's representative to God. Stone notes that the name ***Elohim*** denotes, "strength ... *for* ... great deliverance,"[4] and relates to Christ as the **Priest** who by means of the incarnation in the most perfect sense identifies himself with man. But not only is Jesus identified as the ultimate Priest in his Person, he is also identified as such by his perfect *works* on our behalf.

Most of Jesus Christ's earthly ministry was in fulfillment of his office of Prophet, revealing in Himself the Father and bringing to us the Father's words. But near the end of Jesus' earthly ministry, he began to transition the focus of his work from the Office of Prophet to the Office of Priest. Jesus fulfilled the ultimate priesthood when he took our place on the Cross in payment for our sin. Not only did he go to Calvary on our behalf, but as the Old Testament prophet Isaiah prophesied, and the New Testament writer to the Hebrews affirmed, Jesus as the great High Priest also lives on to make intercession for us! (**Isaiah 53:12; Hebrews 7:25**[5]) Therefore, from the time of his suffering and crucifixion, up until this very moment and until his glorious return, Jesus is primarily functioning in and fulfilling his Office of Priest. That is why the Apostle Paul can both ask and answer the question: "*Who is he that condemneth? It is Christ that died, yea rather, that is risen again, who is even at the right hand of God, who also maketh intercession for us,*" (**Romans 8:34**).

Jesus Christ's divine aid provided for in his perfect **Priesthood** provides for us through faith and obedience, perpetual cleansing, forgiveness, sanctification, and intercession; the ultimate provision for a healthy **progressive** salvation.

C. Christ the King

A king is one who rules for the purpose of establishing and preserving a safe, prosperous and enduring kingdom. *Adonai* equates God as the owner, master, and sovereign of the universe, and corresponds to the office of Christ as **King**.

Virtually all Bible commentators agree that the Gospel of Matthew presents Jesus as Israel's promised messianic King. This is so not only because he is presented and proclaimed as the King, but in large part also because his *power* as king is revealed in his miracles. In his Open Bible introductory commentary of Matthew, (referring to chapters 8 through 11 of Matthew's Gospel), Kenneth Boa states:

"The works of the Lord are presented in a series of ten miracles … that reveal His authority over every realm (disease, demons, death, and nature). Thus the words of the Lord are supported by His works; His claims are verified by His credentials."[6]

Although the Gospel of Matthew presents and authenticates Jesus as the King, the total fulfillment of his Office of King will not occur until his return in power and great glory (**Matthew 24:30; Mark 13:26; Luke 21:27**). But for now, we are promised the protections of a king as we rely daily on Jesus' uttered assurances. Matthew's Gospel records Jesus' very last words as, "…*lo, I am with you alway, even unto the end of the world*" (**Matthew 28:20**). But it is at his Second Coming that Jesus will in the fullest sense operate in his Office of King.

Jesus won and earned his Kingdom at Calvary, and the Kingdom was given to Him at the end of his earthly ministry. After his resurrection and just before his ascension, Jesus declared these words, "*All power is given unto me in heaven and in earth,*" (**Matthew 28:18b**). Although Jesus was *given* the kingdom at the conclusion of his earthly ministry, He has not yet returned to *claim* his Kingdom. He will do so at the Second Coming. It is at that time when Jesus will rescue His redeemed, overthrow Satan, purge the earth of sin and corruption, and establish the Millennial Kingdom with his saints. Satan's third and desperate final temptation of Christ was to offer Him an easier way to inherit the world's kingdoms apart from God's method (**Matthew 4:8-10**). Satan was successful in beguiling Eve to disobey God and heed his redirection to achieving 'goddess' status with only two statements (**Genesis 3:1-6**). But he had no such success with Jesus who fulfilled His mission to the fullest. The Apostle John records the announcement of the great voices in heaven occurring immediately after the seventh trumpet sounded, that said: "…*The kingdoms of this world are become the kingdoms of our Lord, and of his Christ; and He shall reign for ever and ever,*" (**Revelation 11:15b**). If this taking possession of the world kingdoms, as recorded in the book of Revelation, is correctly understood in the 'futuristic' sense, then that physical possession has yet to occur. When **King** Jesus at His second coming does take that possession, it will be the beginning of our **permanent** (*or fully experienced*) salvation.

Reformed theology most often takes a *'preterist'* view of Revelation, which places the divine judgments of Revelation as having already been historically fulfilled at the time when the Jerusalem Temple was destroyed by Rome in A.D. 70. This muddies the theological waters for both the doctrines of eschatology (*end times*) and soteriology (*salvation*). Confusion regarding our permanent salvation is created by the Preterist, despite that both empirical and anecdotal evidence clearly suggests that our post A.D. 70 world has not yet seen the King's final deliverance. Baptists and Pentecostals may disagree on other matters, but generally they both hold the *'futuristic'* view of Revelation.

In sum, Jesus Christ began his earthly ministry as *Prophet*. He continues for us in heaven as our intercessory *Priest*. He is soon coming back as *King* of kings and Lord of lords. Our indescribable, ultimate, and permanent salvation is vested in Jesus Christ who is our protector, who holds our destiny, who will grant us our glorious inheritance, and who will appoint us to co-reign with Him for eternity as a royal priesthood (**1 Peter 2:9; Revelation 1:6**). How great is our God!

CHAPTER SEVEN ENDNOTES

[1] Nathan Stone, *Names of God*, (Chicago: Moody Press, 1944), 20.

[2] *"The LORD thy God will raise up unto thee a Prophet from the midst of thee, of thy brethren, like unto me; unto him ye shall harken,"* (**Deuteronomy 18:15**).

[3] *"Behold, I will send you Elijah the prophet before the coming of the great and dreadful day of the LORD,"* (**Malachi 4:5**).

[4] Stone, 11.

[5] *"...because he hath poured out his soul unto death: and he was numbered with the transgressors; and he bore the sin of many, and made intercession for the transgressors,"* (**Isaiah 53:12b**); *"Wherefore he is able also to save them to the uttermost that come unto God by him, seeing he ever liveth to make intercession for them,"* (**Hebrews 7:25**).

[6] Kenneth D. Boa, *The Open Bible – Study Aids*, (Nashville: Thomas Nelson Publishers, 1985), 938.

CHAPTER 8
THE THREE-FOLD WORK OF THE HOLY SPIRIT

"And when he is come, he will reprove the world of sin, and of
righteousness, and of judgment:
Of sin, because they believe not on me;
Of righteousness, because I go to my Father, and ye see me no more;
Of judgment, because the prince of this world is judged."
John 16:8-11

Elwood McQuaid, in his book *The Outpouring*, asserts that, "Pentecost would herald an age unequaled in the history of mankind since the Fall."[1] This is so, according to McQuaid, because the Church era would be the unique time in the history of mankind when, joined by both Father and Son, "The Holy Spirit, the third person of the Trinity, was to be the indweller of the saints."[2]

McQuaid elaborates from the Gospel of **John** that this indwelling would produce several three-fold blessings:

1. The believer's experiencing of God's *omnipotence* (operative saving, supplying, and sustaining resources of the Godhead), His *omniscience* (direction for daily living), and His *omnipresence* (the Lord of Glory, tabernacled in every believing sinner on earth and in heaven);

2. The believers become the beneficiaries of *divine instruction* (taught, and brought to remembrance what Jesus said by the Spirit; **14:26**), of *divine guidance* (into all truth by the Spirit; **16:13**), and of *divine illumination* (showing of things heard and of things to come by the Spirit; **16:13**);

3. All this resulting in a *life of love* (by the Spirit's imparting of the capacity to love one another; **15:9-14**), a *life of joy* (by the Spirit's opening of God's storehouse so that we may ask and receive, and our joy may be full; **16:22-24**), and a *life of peace* (by the Spirit's provision of inner peace, unlike that of the world; **14:27**).

McQuaid concludes from the above observations of the Gospel of **John** that this life in the Spirit is one of *privileged position* (**15:12-16**), *constructive separation* (unto Christ, **15:18-27**), and *perpetual fruit-bearing* (**15:1-8**).[3] Indeed, following the first coming of Jesus Christ on the earth, the Spirit's coming and work during the Church Age is an unparalleled 'divine intrusion' by God into the affairs of men. It is so, in that we, the heirs of God, can be empowered by the provision of divinely-procured resources, by which we are enabled to live triumphantly in this life.

A. Of Sin

The Holy Spirit's conviction of sin is the very first step leading us to salvation. Without conviction there can be no belief, no true confession, and no repentance. Without repentance there can be no forgiveness. Without forgiveness there is no salvation. For man to look to God for salvation, his unbelief requires conviction of sin.

In seeing again how many three-dimensional truths are embedded in and attributed to the Gospel, Paul Enns offers this observation about sin and saving faith, as it relates to the tri-part soul of man;

"Saving faith, however, is not mere intellectual assent to a doctrine; it involves more than that. Saving faith involves at least three elements.

1) Knowledge - This involves the *intellect*... believing the basic truths fundamental to man's salvation: man's sinfulness, Christ's atoning sacrifice, and His bodily resurrection...

2) <u>Conviction</u> - …involves the *emotions*… an inner conviction (*of sin*)… and

3) <u>Trust</u> - …a moving of the *will*."[4]

The Holy Spirit's primary work is the convicting of an unbelieving world, of sin. Enns describes it as, "…the work of a prosecuting attorney whereby He seeks to convince someone of something. The Holy Spirit acts as a divine prosecutor, convicting the world of sin because of its refusal to believe in Jesus."[5]

In his Commentary on the Holy Bible, Matthew Henry argues that unbelief is, "…at the bottom of all sin. … The awakened sinner begins to perceive that unbelief arises from pride, love of sin, and enmity to God; that it is the source, and, as it were, the substance of all other sins."[6]

Without recognition of sin, man is utterly lost because he does not appreciate his need to seek remedy for his condition. Only the Holy Spirit can provide this conviction that leads to the awakening of faith in God's provision of salvation. This recognition cannot come from a purely intellectual understanding of the general concept of sin. It must be personalized and internalized, producing an urgent desire for escape from sin and its consequences.

In this New Testament era of grace, man is blessed to have the Holy Spirit active in the work of conviction of sin without which no man can be saved. Man is blessed that the Holy Spirit is ready to regenerate and indwell those who respond to His convicting power by their willingness to place their faith in Christ. The unsaved man is already under God's condemnation (**John 3:18-21**). As the Holy Spirit convicts, the responsive believing man is saved and is no longer under condemnation (**Romans 8:1**).

This sin-convicting work of the Holy Spirit focuses primarily on bringing sinful man to a confrontation of his spiritual need, and the realization that in Christ he can receive ***positional salvation*** through the regeneration of his spirit. He does this by illumination; unveiling for us the utter *sinfulness* of sin, the perfect *righteousness* of God of which we can be partakers, and the absolute *holiness* of God which demands judgment.

B. Of Righteousness

The term *righteousness* has been aptly defined as God's perfect conformity to all of His divine attributes. Because God is perfectly righteous, he cannot prefer or isolate any one of His attributes over another. Therefore, God's *justice* is always in perfect balance with his *mercy*. His *holiness* is in perfect harmony with his *long-suffering*. As is His *truth* with His *grace*. When we prefer or isolate one of God's attributes over another, we fall into imbalance, wrong doctrine, and unrighteousness. Appropriately, Marvin Rosenthal defines *unrighteousness* as, "the committing of acts that do not conform to God's character."[7]

The Holy Spirit's work in reproving men of righteousness is crucial for the recognition of Jesus Christ as the only able Savior. Jesus said, "*Nevertheless I tell you the truth; It is expedient for you that I go away: for if I go not away, the Comforter will not come unto you; but if I depart, I will send him unto you*" (**John 16:7**). The Holy Spirit did not come to draw attention to Himself (**John 16:13**), but rather, to "*Jesus Christ the Righteous*" (**1 John 2:1**). In this vein of thought, the Apostle John also said, "*He that speaketh of himself seeketh his own glory: but he that seeketh his glory that sent him, the same is true, and no unrighteousness is in him*" (**John 7:18**). Jesus came to bring us the words of his Father. The Holy Spirit came to guide us "*into all truth*" and to glorify Jesus Christ (**John 16:13-14**). He does so by convincing men of the righteousness of the ascended Christ.

By exalting Jesus Christ and his righteousness, the Holy Spirit points all men unto Christ according to the Father's will. We then become the benefactors of righteousness. The Apostle Paul writes to the Corinthians, "*For he (God the Father) hath made him (Jesus Christ) to be sin for us, who knew no sin; that we might be made the righteousness of God in him,*" (**2 Corinthians 5:21**). We are imputed with the righteousness of Christ (**Romans 4**)!

Our desire and aim as believers should then be, to be more and more like Him (*Jesus Christ*). In fact, the Apostle Paul, when writing to the Romans, predicts our ultimate destiny when he proclaims, "*For whom he did foreknow, he also did predestinate to be conformed to the image of his Son, that he might be the firstborn among many brethren,"* (**Romans 8:29**).

One of the disciplines of the Faith that has largely fallen out of practice in modern Christianity is 'prayer and fasting.' The effectiveness of proper fasting (undergirded by prayer) is that it strengthens our spirit while simultaneously weakening the carnality of our flesh. **Isaiah 58** speaks to both, how God rejects the hollow practice of self-righteous religious fasting, and how He causes blessings to flow from proper fasting. **Isaiah 58:6** declares that the fast that God calls for, produces four things: it **1)** loosens the bands of wickedness; **2)** lightens heavy burdens; **3)** frees the oppressed; and **4)** breaks every yoke. Rebuking the unbelief of his disciples, in **Matthew 17:17-21**, Jesus drew a direct spiritual contrast between 'faithlessness' & 'perverseness,' and 'prayer' & 'fasting.' Jesus was teaching that *prayer* (undergirded by His Word) is God's prescription for faithlessness, because prayer draws us closer to God and energizes our faith. Likewise, *fasting* is God's prescription for perverseness, because it loosens our connection to worldliness that fuels perversion and sin. What we feed the most is what grows the most! Prayer feeds the spirit to strengthen our faith, and fasting starves the flesh to weaken the pull to sin.

Until the time of glorification comes when we are eternally perfected by Jesus Christ at His Second Coming, we are to strive for personal holiness and godliness to the glory of God. We are not left to ourselves in this pursuit. We are aided by the Holy Spirit, our Comforter. Without His help we would labor in vain in the pursuit of righteousness. Paul exhorted as follows, *"For if ye live after the flesh, ye shall die: but if ye through the Spirit do mortify the deeds of the body, ye shall live"* (**Romans 8:13**).

This convicting work of the Holy Spirit unto righteousness focuses primarily on bringing the redeemed man to increased sanctification and ***progressive salvation*** through the fortification of his soul.

C. Of Judgment

The *"prince of this world"* is clearly identified as Satan. Subsequent to the Triumphal Entry into Jerusalem, when Jesus began to prepare the disciples for his impending death, the Father for the third time authenticated his Son with an audible voice from heaven (1st **Matthew 3:17;** 2nd **Matthew 17:5;** 3rd **John 12:28**). As a follow-up to God's third affirming audible voice, Jesus declared, *"Now is the judgment of this world: now shall the prince of this world be cast out"* (**John 12:31**).

Jesus' declaration concerning judgment was in reference to his Resurrection, as the ultimate turning point in the conflict of the ages. Satan maneuvered through the ages in his futile attempts to prevent and/or kill the 'Seed of the woman' for the purpose of thwarting the will of God to save mankind and ultimately crush his (*Satan's*) head. This conflict between God and Satan that has raged on over the ages began in the Garden of Eden. After man's fall, God declared that a contest between the 'seed of the serpent' and the 'seed of the woman' would conclude at the end of the age, when the Seed of the woman (Jesus Christ) would ultimately destroy the seed of the serpent (**Genesis 3:15**).[8]

This raging conflict between God and Satan continued after the Garden encounter through each era of mankind:

- Shortly after the Fall, Adam's godly son Abel was murdered by his evil-inspired brother Cain (**Genesis 4:8,17-26**).[9] This was Satan's first volley in the great ongoing conflict. But God countered by raising godly seed through Seth and Enoch.

- When the world initially began to be populated, Satan tried again to prevent the seed of the woman from eventually emerging, with a scheme to pollute mankind's gene pool through the copulation of demonic beings with human women (**Genesis 6:2**).[10] This would have resulted in the reproduction of generations of mongrel people with demonically tainted DNA, resulting in the ultimate prevention of Jesus' necessary "hypostatic union," (Jesus, the perfect 'God-man'). Jesus' imperfect humanity would render him unable to save us. God, separating Noah (and his family), *"perfect in his generations"* (**Genesis 6:9**), meaning that Noah's lineage had not yet been contaminated by Satan's attack on mankind's human genetic makeup, then purged the world of this Satanic pollution of humanity through the Flood.

- After the Flood, to lure men away from God, Nimrod introduced the world to an astrology-based false religious system (**Genesis**

11:4).[11] The worship of planets and other idols as gods/goddesses has through the ages been a powerful diversion. Will Durant, in his work on the history of civilization said of astrology, "Even the Jews, the least superstitious of all people, expressed good wishes by saying 'Mazzol-Tov'

- – 'May your planet be favorable'."[12] This ancient birth of astrology is the foundation for the historical and contemporary cults and New Age-type movements.

In this conflict, Satan not only tried to corrupt and lure away mankind, but he also attempted through infertility, corrupt leadership, and successive world powers to prevent the promised "seed" from ever emerging on the face of the earth. The Patriarchs Abraham's, Isaac's, and Jacob's wives were all barren. After escaping from famine into Egypt, a succeeding Pharaoh sought to wipe the infant nation of Jews off the face of the earth. In order to clear the way for succession to the Judean throne as the first (and only) Queen, evil Athaliah killed off the "*seed royal*" (**2 Kings 11:1**; **2 Chronicles 22:10**). So did Nebuchadnezzar of the Babylonians, when he dethroned Judah's King Zedekiah, the last 'legitimate' King of Judah from the Davidic lineage. In Zedekiah's presence, Nebuchadnezzar killed all of his heirs and then plucked out his eyes, so that the last thing Zedekiah saw was his royal lineage being cut off (**2 Kings 25:7**). As recorded in the Old Testament book of **Esther** (**3:5-6**), Haman of the Persians also devised a plot to kill all Jews during the exile. Not to be outdone, during the inter-testament "400 silent years," Antiochus 'Epiphanes' IV of the Syrians, who came to power in 175 B.C., intended to destroy the Jewish race. With an aim to plunder and force Jews into forsaking their God, he defiled the Temple by setting himself up in it as a god. Will Durant says of Antiochus, "He enjoyed his own qualities so keenly that he labeled his coins Antiochus Theos Epiphanes – The God Made Manifest."[13]

Many more examples of Satan's attempts to disrupt God's plan through the seed of the woman could be offered. Not the least being during the Roman Empire, when shortly after the birth of Jesus, King Herod's decree to kill all little Jewish boys, two years old and under, was intended by Satan as a desperate effort to prevent the newly born "Seed" from living long enough to fulfill his mission (**Matthew 2:16**[14];

Revelation 12:4). Satan then tried to tempt Jesus, weakened from His 40-day fast, to defect to him so to forfeit His ordination as the promised 'Seed of the woman' (**Matthew 4:1-11**). Later, in the 'nick of time,' Satan thought he had finally won the decisive victory over the "Seed" at the Cross, by inspiring the Jewish religious leaders and Roman authorities to successfully kill Jesus (**Luke 23:46**). But Satan was set back once again by the Resurrection! In much more recent history, Adolph Hitler's demonically inspired Nazi Germany did all they could to eliminate Jews (*the lineage from which the 'woman's seed' came*), from the face of the earth.

For the sake of brevity, the above examples should suffice to trace the trail highlights of Satan's tenacious fixation and efforts at trying to preserve himself by attempting to outmaneuver God. For every one of Satan's moves, God countered with a means to preserve his promised Seed and the hope for all mankind. Marvin Rosenthal is one who has popularized calling this 'move and counter-move' contest, the "Conflict of the Ages." In a message entitled "The Plan of Salvation," Evangelist Tony Evans described it as a "Cosmic Chess Game."

Because *Soul Baptism* attempts to highlight the Bible's three-dimensional truths, let me here briefly illustrate an eschatological (end-time) teaching of Jesus where He connects together three events to shed light on an important element for His Church to understand concerning the last-days. Jesus taught that the (second) coming of the Son of Man would be "*as the days of Noe* (Noah) *were,*" and "*Likewise also as it was in the days of Lot*" (**Matthew 24:37**; **Luke 17:26-30**). Jesus ties in these three events; the time of Noah, the time of Lot, and the 'last days.' What is the connection? The Satanic defilement of mankind through some sort of an intimate relationship of bonding between Satan and mankind.

As already outlined above, in Noah's day Satan used his demons in the attempt to contaminate the human gene pool. God purged that effort with the global Flood. In Lot's day, the Satanically deceived and completely depraved men of Sodom and Gomorrah violently demanded to engage in sexual relations with the visiting angels. Even after being blinded by the angels, they persisted to exhaustion as they "*wearied themselves to find the door*" (**Genesis 19:4-11**). God destroyed

Sodom and Gomorrah by raining down "*brimstone and fire*" from heaven (**Genesis 19:24**). In the last days, satanic beings will again in some way attempt to "*mingle themselves with the seed of men*" (**Daniel 2:43**). This imagery of Daniel has connection with the end-time "*666*" 'Mark of the Beast' (**Revelation 13:16-18, 14:9-11**), where the Antichrist will impose all men to receive his mark of union with him. Those who comply will suffer the torment of "*fire and brimstone in the presence of the holy angels, and in the presence of the Lamb.*"

The Holy Spirit's third role in the **John 16:8-11** passage, is to highlight God's uncompromised holiness which can do nothing else but conclude in the sure judgment of all sin and unrighteousness. It points to the end result of man's ultimate state of *permanent salvation*.

Chapter Eight Endnotes

[1] Elwood McQuaid, *The Outpouring*, (Bellmawr, NJ: The Friends of Israel Gospel Ministry, 1990), 143.

[2] McQuaid, 143.

[3] McQuaid, 143-144.

[4] Enns, 332.

[5] Enns, 140.

[6] Henry, Volume III, 405.

[7] Marvin Rosenthal, *The Pre-Wrath Rapture of the Church*, (Nashville: Thomas Nelson Publishers, 1990), 163.

[8] *"And I will put enmity between thee and the woman, and between thy seed and her seed; it shall bruise thy head, and thou shalt bruise his heel,"* (**Genesis 3:15**).

[9] *"And Cain talked with Abel his brother: and it came to pass, when they were in the field, that Cain rose up against Abel his brother, and slew him,"* (**Genesis 4:8**).

[10] *"That the sons of God saw the daughters of men that they were fair; and they took them wives of all which they chose,"* (**Genesis 6:2**).

[11] *"And they said, Go to, let us build us a city and a tower, whose top may reach unto heaven; and let us make us a name, lest we be scattered abroad upon the face of the whole earth,"* (**Genesis 11:4**).

[12] Will Durant, *The Story of Civilization: Part II*, (New York: Simon & Schuster, 1939), 566.

[13] Durant, 574.

[14] *"Then Herod, when he saw that he was mocked of the wise men, was exceeding wroth, and sent forth, and slew all the children that were in Bethlehem, and in all the coasts thereof, from two years old and under, according to the time which he had diligently inquired of the wise men,"* (**Matthew 2:16**).

Chapter 9
The Baptism with the Holy Spirit

"But ye shall receive power, after that the Holy Ghost is come upon you: and ye shall be witnesses unto me both in Jerusalem, and in all Judea and in Samaria, and unto the uttermost part of the earth."
Acts 1:8

What is the baptism with the Holy Spirit? Most Baptistic and "main-line" Reformed Protestants will argue that there is only one "Spirit baptism." Their view is that ever since Pentecost (**Acts 2**), this baptism occurs at the moment of conversion and is regenerational unto salvation. At that initial moment of salvation, the believer receives all the Holy Spirit and spiritual giftings that God has to offer for his Christian lifetime on the earth. According to this view, there is no subsequent post-salvation supernatural spiritual experience that can be added to the regenerated believer's life. Seeking a subsequent spiritual experience is, in the Reformed and Baptistic minds, unnecessary, in error, possibly blasphemous, and perhaps even dangerously demonic!

Commenting on the doctrine of **Subsequence** (*the Pentecostal view that the baptism with the Holy Spirit is a subsequent experience to regeneration – "subsequence" is further discussed later in this chapter*), John MacArthur asserts that charismatics come dangerously close to the abominable error of the Simon "the Sorcerer" of **Acts 8:9-24**. In *Charismatic Chaos*, MacArthur states:

> "Charismatics…thirst for something more, the quest for greater power, and the desire to see evidences that are as familiar today as they were in Corinth. Yet they are more compatible with the spirit of Simon than with the Spirit of God."[1]

The Pentecostal view agrees with the Reformed and Baptistic position that all true Christians have been *born of* the Spirit. But it differs, in that the Pentecostal believes not all have been subsequently *baptized **with*** the Spirit. The Pentecostal will argue that the baptism *with* the Holy Spirit is not for the unregenerate's rebirth, but rather as an additional aid for the already born-again Christian's enablement for service.

Isaiah exhorted God's people to set aside error and seek doctrinal truth. How? "*Precept upon precept, line upon line… here a little, and there a little.*" He even spoke of "*stammering lips and another tongue*" and of "*refreshing*" that God would teach to His erring people and their scornful leaders, "*yet they would not hear*" (**Isaiah 28:9-14**). In this respect, Paul argued that tongues are a sign for unbelievers (**1 Corinthians 14:22**).

Though the following pages will elaborate somewhat on 'tongues,' the purpose of this book is not to judge the strengths and weaknesses of the opposing theological arguments surrounding this issue, nor to offer an extensive debate over *glossolalia* ('*tongues' speaking*). The goal is to piece truth together from the various passages of related Scripture, to help all sides see the subject at hand from the Biblical three-dimensional perspective, so that unnecessary schisms may be bridged.

A. Definition of the Baptism *with* the Holy Spirit

Regretfully, there is no shortage of contention and ridicule on this issue towards believers of Pentecostal persuasion from those of non-Pentecostal denominations. But, it is interesting to note that the topic has often been misunderstood by both Pentecostals and non-Pentecostals alike! This is so, because at times positions are taken based on tradition, personal experiences, suggestion, inaccurate definition of terms, and/or a loose, inconsistent, or erroneous understanding and interpretation of God's Word.

On the Day of Pentecost, the Apostles and believers, 120 of them, who obeying Jesus' Ascension Day instructions to tarry in Jerusalem until empowered by the 'Father's Promise' (**Luke 24:49**), were united in an upper room. They were already saved and indwelt by the Spirit in the New Testament sense, because as His first order of Church business on Resurrection Day, fifty days prior to Pentecost, Jesus had already put the 'born-again' process in place by transferring the breath of the Holy Spirit within them (**John 20:22**). So, on this Pentecost Sunday, suddenly, the powerful presence of God filled the room and the 120 were filled (*baptized*) with the Holy Spirit. This infilling caused them to miraculously begin to speak in foreign languages that they had never studied or learned, as the Spirit inspired their utterance (**Acts 2:1-4**). This outburst of 'tongues worship' occurred internally at the meeting, but was also overheard and taken notice of by others outside of their immediate upper room location. Pentecost was one of the Feasts that required Jews to gather and celebrate at the Jerusalem Temple, so on that day there were visiting Jews lodging in Jerusalem from "*every nation under heaven*" (**Acts 2:7**). The tongues utterance was not a communication to each other, nor preaching directed at others, it was a Spirit-inspired worship to God of praise for His "*wonderful works*" (**Acts 2:11**)! When the astonished outsiders inquired, Peter began to preach Christ to them. Peter explained that this was the fulfillment of Old Testament prophecy that in the last days (*Church Age*), God would pour out His Spirit (*manifestational giftings*) upon all peoples (**Acts 2:17; Joel 2:28-29**).

Peter further explained that what they were seeing and hearing was the fulfillment of the 'Father's Promise,' sent by the ascended Jesus who had received it from the Father in heaven for the Church (**Acts 2:33**). When conviction came upon the hearts of the hearers of Peter's preaching, they asked what they should do in response to this message. Peter exhorted them to repent, trust Christ for the remission of their sins, and be (*water*) baptized. They, and all Church Age generations to follow, would then become eligible to receive this promised gift of the Holy Ghost. 3,000 of them responded that day (**Acts 2:37-41**).

The Baptism with the Holy Spirit is a basic ministry/manifestational gift of empowerment promised by God to the Church, sent to believers by the ascended Christ, and manifesting in the receiving believers through the Spirit. Most will conclude that the initial outward 'evidence' of having received this gift is the manifestation of a 'tongues' utterance. The longer-term benefit of this gift is greater empowerment to serve Christ. Cessationists try their hardest to redefine 'tongues-speaking' as a motivational 'aptitude' gift that grants an individual an enhanced natural ability to more quickly learn a foreign language as an aid towards fulfilling the Great Commission through foreign missions work. But, as further discussed in this chapter under the "Evidence" heading, sometimes the 'tongues' utterance is "*unknown,*" and understood by no person on earth, only God (**1 Corinthians 14:2**)!

Contrary to many wrongful assumptions and criticisms of this 'Pentecostal baptism,' offered mostly by those who do not understand it, or have never experienced or even witnessed it in its genuine gifting by the Spirit, the baptism *with* the Spirit is a real and Biblically authentic spiritual gift! Allow me to first say what the 'baptism with the Holy Spirit' is not. While, like every gift of God, it is given by grace and not merit, it's not a 'second work of grace' unto sanctification, perfection, or sinlessness of the faithful. Nor is it even a new capacity or empowerment to 'sin less,' beyond the exhortations of **Galatians 5:16**! I've heard some Pentecostals erroneously suggest that 'eternal security' attaches to the believer only after that believer receives the baptism with the Holy Spirit with the evidence of speaking in tongues. This is just a poor attempt at trying to reconcile what appear as incompatible doctrines! Simply speaking, what this baptism is, is an encounter of spiritual intimacy with Christ through the Spirit that produces an initial manifestation of spiritual comfort and empowerment, and a long-term effect that often enables one to minister more profoundly above his or her natural means. It's an undeniable touch of God that forever changes the recipient, though he's still vulnerable to the flesh, and required to walk by faith and in all the disciplines of the Faith.

My approach to further defining the baptism with the Holy Spirit will be to touch on three areas: The Baptizer; The Apostles; and The Evidence.

1) The Baptizer

One seemingly minor, but relevant point that speaks to this discussion is the terminology that's used when referring to the baptism **with** the Holy Spirit. All too often the 'Pentecostal' baptism is misstated as a baptism *of*, or *by*, or *in*, or *into* the Spirit. In all major translations, to include the historically most commonly used Authorized King James Version, as well as the Revised Standard, and the New International versions, the preposition used by John the Baptist, Jesus Christ, and the Apostle Peter, is *"with"* when referring to what the Pentecostals define as the subsequent Spirit baptism, (**Mark 1:8, Acts 1:5** and **11:16**).[2] *Strong's Exhaustive Concordance and Greek Dictionary* ascribe for "*with*," the Greek word number 4862 (which is defined as; "a prim. prep. denoting *union*; *with* or *together* [but much closer than 3326 or 3844], i.e., by association, companionship, process, resemblance, possession, instrumentality, addition, etc.: - beside, with. In comp. it has similar applications, includ. *completeness*.")[3] The other related terms referred to by *Strong's*, (3326 and 3844), are defined as much weaker and more casual in their association.

We shall see later that in the Book of Acts the baptism with the Holy Spirit is also described by such terms as, "filled," "falling upon," "poured on," and "came on" (**Acts 2:4, 10:44-45, 19:6**). Regardless of how the giving of the baptism with the Holy Spirit is described, it had to by faith be willingly *received* by the recipients (**Acts 10:47**). The Holy Spirit does not force Himself upon the eligible New Testament believers.

The importance for the distinction in the preposition used relates to the clarifying point that there are different baptisms. In Chapter 2, the suggestion offered was that there are three distinct Christian baptisms. The baptism *by* the Spirit *into* one body (**1 Corinthians 12:13**)[4] clearly refers to the baptism of regeneration unto salvation placing believers into the "Body of Christ" which is the "Church," the Kingdom body of all regenerated believers. All three major Bible translations mentioned above use the same terms, *by* and *into* for this verse. On this issue, even what has been the most popular paraphrase, The Living Bible, follows suit on the prepositional uses of *with*, *by*, and *into*.

As was mentioned at the end of Chapter 4, it is essential to again note here that the threshold from Old Testament salvation to New Testament salvation was crossed over on Resurrection Day by the resurrected Jesus, 40 days prior to His ascension, and 50 days prior to the Pentecost outpouring. By His initial breathing of the Holy Spirit of regeneration into the disciples, and stating, *"Receive ye the Holy Ghost,"* (**John 20:22b**), Jesus set in motion the New Testament experience of being, *"born of the Spirit,"* (**John 3:8b**). The disciples' spirits were at that moment regenerated in the New Testament sense. These were the first to experience being 'born-again' by the Spirit of God. Jesus set in motion the "breath," and from that moment forward, the 'Baptizer' unto regeneration (according to **1 Corinthians 12:13**), is the Holy Spirit. On every believer since that initial breathing by Jesus, and continuing past His ascension, the rebirth baptism of regeneration is performed *by* the **Holy Spirit**.

Water baptism, or 'believer's baptism' as the Baptists term it, is the second Christian baptism and it is generally performed by a duly authorized Christian minister. In the "Great Commission" (**Matthew 28:19-20**)[5], Jesus sent his apostles to go forth and preach the Gospel to the whole world and to water-baptize those who believe and confess Christ unto salvation. The baptizer in water is therefore a **human minister**. Because the Church sometimes mis-prioritizes its evangelistic focus, I must emphasize here that the Great Commission was not given to merely go and recruit new *converts*, but rather to make *disciples*, by baptizing and *teaching* believers who come to faith in Christ.

But in the discussion of the third baptism *with* the Spirit, the baptizer is identified as **Jesus Christ**, not the Holy Spirit, nor a human minister. God will always reveal or give a foretaste to His prophets of something previously hidden that He's about to do (**Amos 3:7**). As the Forerunner, who in a sense was the first recipient to foretaste of this baptism with the Spirit from the yet pre-born (*and obviously pre-ascended*) Jesus (**Luke 1:15,41,44**), John the Baptist is uniquely qualified to be the first to identify Jesus as the baptizer *with* the Holy Spirit (**Matthew 3:11,14**[6]; **John 1:32-33**) We must acknowledge the empowering baptism *with* the Spirit as the "promise of the Father," (**Acts 1:4**). It was initiated and given by the Father, but it is Jesus who receiving it from the Father, became the administrator of the gift to us (**John 16:7,15; Acts 2:33**). The Father *gave* it. The Son *directs* it. The Spirit *applies* it.

It is then quite indisputable that the three baptisms are administered by three distinct "Individuals." The baptism *by* the <u>Holy Spirit</u> is unto regeneration. Water baptism by a <u>human minister</u> is for the believer's obedience and identification with Christ. The baptism *with* the Holy Spirit administered by <u>Jesus</u> is for empowerment, enablement, or equipping. As stated above, Jesus' first 'prototype' of this baptism was from Mary's womb unto pre-born John the Baptist who would not live to see Pentecost. Then ten days after the Ascension, it was dispensed to the 120 at Pentecost. The eleven timid disciples who withdrew, and Peter who three times denied knowing Jesus after His (Jesus') arrest, were clearly emboldened after Pentecost. After that, both Jewish and Gentile believers received this gift. It is further promised to all "*afar off*" generations, "*even as many as the Lord our God shall call*" (**Acts 2:39**). Not only is salvation available to subsequent generations, but also the promise of availability for the life-changing spiritual intimacy experience that empowers believers!

No 'Spirit-filled' Christian, Baptist, or Reformed believer should ever be arrogant, self-righteous, or convey an air of spiritual superiority. This was at times the sin of the Israelites who felt themselves superior as sons of Abraham, Issac, and Jacob, and as God's 'chosen race.' Both John the Baptist and Jesus called the Jews out on this (**Matthew 3:9; Luke 3:8; John 8:39**). Jesus drew further attention to this error of arrogance by comparing the attitude of the Pharisee toward the humble publican, when both were praying in the Temple (**Luke 18:10-14**). Rather, the Spirit causes the mature believer to understand with humility his own insufficiency apart from the Spirit of God who enables him. Because God sovereignly dispenses His gifts by grace, and not by merit, He emphasized this point dramatically by extravagantly showering His manifestational giftings to the Corinthian church, who all agree was the most immature, carnal, and flawed church of the New Testament!

2) The Apostles

Again, one of the foundational principles undergirding the Pentecostal doctrine of the baptism *with* the Holy Spirit is **Subsequence**.

One way of explaining this doctrine is that the candidate for the baptism *with* the Spirit must first be regenerated, or already 'born again.' This Spirit-baptism is therefore *subsequent* to the regenerational-baptism unto salvation. This is based on Jesus' teaching from the Gospel of John where he stresses the point that the Comforter cannot be received by the world because it doesn't know him, (**John 14:16-17**).[7]

By contrast, every baptism of regeneration into the Body of Christ is effected onto those in the world, who up to that moment of regeneration had not known him! In that **John 14** passage it is suggested that the believing disciples already knew the Spirit because He abided *with* them, but would later be *in* them. We established that the Spirit entered into the disciples at the time the resurrected Jesus, on Resurrection Day (50 days <u>prior</u> to Pentecost), breathed on them to receive the Holy Spirit, thereby producing the New Testament spiritual rebirth.

By the time Pentecost came, the Spirit was already in them in the New Testament regenerational sense, and Jesus was now ascended. Jesus had told his disciples that it was critical he be ascended into heaven or the Comforter could not come, (**John 16:7**).[8] Therefore the baptism with the Holy Spirit received on the day of Pentecost was <u>not</u> for the disciples' rebirth. It was clearly for their empowerment to be able to effectively carry out the Great Commission.

It is also important to consider how the early Apostles understood the baptism *with* the Holy Spirit. It's inconceivable that the original disciples, renamed 'Apostles,' who had been personally taught and trained by Jesus, who had been sent out as advance-teams and ministry-teams by Jesus, who then witnessed his crucifixion, death, resurrection, ascension, and Pentecost, would themselves at this advanced point in time fumble the most elementary basics, or allow their fellow ministers to do so without clear and immediate correction.

One of those basics was water-baptism. The Christian conversion water baptism was to be administered only to those who *after* believing the Gospel and repenting of their sins, professed faith in Jesus Christ unto regeneration. No early Apostle would have performed or tolerated water baptism for an unbeliever. Even today, all Bible-believing Christians agree that water baptism is only properly administered to believers who have confessed having received saving grace through Christ. All agree that water-baptism doesn't save – it is administered to affirm *outwardly* the salvation that has already taken place *inwardly*! It is one of the very first steps of obedience for the newly converted believer. If the baptism with the Holy Spirit is to be equated with regeneration, and not as a subsequent-to-salvation experience, then the basic rule of water baptism, which is to be performed only on the already regenerate, was not the consistent pattern in the book of Acts and the early Apostles grossly erred…

Consider the following:

a) In **Acts 2**, the 120 believers were not water-baptized after their baptism with the Spirit on the day of Pentecost;

b) In **Acts 8**, Peter and John went to Samaria because a revival had broken out through the ministry of Philip. The Samaritans were being healed of diseases, delivered from demonic possession, and were evidencing the joy of salvation. They believed the Word of God and were being water baptized in the name of the Lord Jesus. Yet Peter and John were sent to lay hands on them to receive the baptism with the Holy Spirit because, "*as yet he was fallen upon none of them*" (**8:16**);

c) Similarly, in **Acts 19**, the Holy Spirit came on the Ephesian disciples subsequent to their belief *and* water baptism;

d) Another example is **Acts 10:45-47**. Peter and his Jewish companions were astonished that the Holy Spirit was poured out on Cornelius and the believing Gentiles with him because they witnessed the same outward 'tongue' evidences of having received the baptism with the Holy Spirit that the believing Jews had initially experienced at Pentecost (**Acts 11:15-17**). Based on this evidence, they could find no reason to withhold water baptism from them because having received the 'subsequent' baptism proved in their minds that these gentiles must have already, nearly simultaneously, been regenerated by God, rendering them worthy candidates for water baptism.

3) The Evidence

Most Pentecostals believe that the initial physical sign or 'outward evidence' that a person has received the subsequent-to-salvation baptism *with* the Holy Spirit is the phenomenon of Spirit-prompted *glossolalia,* i.e., 'tongues.' In the broader sense, the gift of *"divers kinds of tongues"* (**1 Corinthians 12:10**) is the Holy Spirit prompted utterance in a foreign (*or unknown "angelic"* **1 Corinthians 13:1**) language that the speaker has never learned and does not himself understand. That tongues utterance can be devotional in the private function of worship or prayer, or prophetic for the Body of Christ if in a public setting and interpreted (**1 Corinthians 14:5**). Because of the intimacy of relationship with Christ in the course of the baptism with the Holy Spirit that prompts the utterance from the innermost spirit of man, it is always accompanied by comfort, joy, and elation of the Holy Ghost (**Acts 13:52**). Nevertheless, the person speaking (worshiping/praying) in *'unknown'* (*i.e., "angelic"*) tongues, who is understood by no one except God, is himself edified (**1 Corinthians 14:2,4**).

'Unknown tongues' is an even more contentious topic of discussion between Pentecostals and 'mainline' believers, than just 'tongues' is! Most cessationist 'main-liners' may, even reluctantly, accept the 'historical,' temporal and now extinct (*they say*), miraculous ability to speak in a previously unlearned *foreign* language as a necessary initial authenticating 'sign' for the founding and expansion of the early Church, but they gag at the idea of 'unknown' tongues utterances. Great men of God, such as some of the ones mentioned in this book, scoff at 'unknown tongues,' calling it pure "gibberish." Why are sincere servants of God sometimes so quick to judge what they may not understand? It reminds me of God's scolding of Job and his three pontificating 'theologian' friends, when He said, *"Who is this that darkeneth counsel by words without knowledge?"* (**Job 38:2**). While there is Scriptural evidence for *'unknown'* tongues, I will ask this empirical-evidence question: Why is it that the often so called *"handala-shandala" gibberish* is so ridiculed, when the phenomenon of the genuine Spirit-prompted unknown-tongue utterance, wherever it's heard spoken in the world, by generations of peoples who have no connection to each other, has such a similar sound in speech patterns and apparent linguistic construct? It's a question well worth considering!

There are three New Testament Biblical terms that distinctly define the miraculous gifts: First there are *"power-miracles,"* or *"mighty works,"* which are remarkable acts that contradict known scientific laws. These are identified in the Greek as ***dunamis*** (Strong's #1411). Then there are "*wonders*," which produce marvel, astonishment and admiration. In the Greek, these are **teras** (Strong's #5059). Finally, there are "*signs*," to signify, mark, or indicate a fact or quality. This is from the Greek **semaino** (Strong's #4591). These three miraculous operations can manifest in a positive manner (**Acts 2:22** – as by Christ), or in a negative manner (**2 Thessalonians 2:9** – as by the Antichrist). For the purpose of this discussion, the Scripture clearly teaches us that the 'baptism with the Holy Spirit' is for empowerment (*'dunamis,'* **Luke 24:49**; **Acts 1:8**), and that, "*tongues are for a sign*" (*'semaino,'* **1 Corinthians 14:22**). Hence, 'tongues' is the Biblically consistent outward 'sign' of having received the baptism with the Holy Spirit.

The purpose of tongues is the edifying Spirit-aided worship, the giving of thanks, and/or praying in the spirit, when our natural language is inadequate to express what the Spirit is stirring within us (**1 Corinthians 14:14-18**). We're required to worship in spirit and in truth (**John 4:24**). Regarding prayer, Paul taught that we all have common "*infirmities*" of not knowing, "*what we should pray for as we ought*" (**Romans 8:26-27**). The Spirit helps us to pray His will (**1 John 5:14**), and to avoid asking "*amiss*" (**James 4:3**). Contextually, it is only when we allow the Spirit to help us with this 'infirmity,' that we can be assured of, "*all things work(ing) together for good*" (**Romans 8:26-28**). The Spirit helps us pray and worship both with our natural abilities of understanding, and through the supernatural gift-enablement of 'tongues' (**1 Corinthians 14:15**).

'Tongues' is one of those doctrines that divides Christians at least as much as those who argue over their understanding of 'free-will' and 'eternal security.' I will attempt to briefly explain why many Pentecostals firmly adhere to their view of tongues as being the manifest evidence of the Spirit's infilling. But in doing so, I will concede that it is a *secondary* issue, in that it is not an essential primary matter related to salvation so that it should become a wedge to divide us. I say it's unessential, not because it's unimportant or insignificant, but because believing or not believing in the "gift of tongues" for today does not keep one from salvation and 'reaching heaven.' I concur on this point with Hank Hanegraaff, who up until a few years ago was the well-known President of the Christian Research Institute and apologist, when he adopts the wise maxim, "In essentials unity; in non-essentials liberty; and in all things charity."[9] In his work entitled, *Counterfeit Revival*, Hanegraaff stated as follows:

> "It should be noted that sincere believers are today divided on the issue of tongues. Some believe that they ceased with the closing of the canon of Scripture or the end of the apostolic age. Others do not see a clear biblical or historical precedent for such a position. While we may vigorously debate the issue of tongues, we must never divide over it."[10]

Truth transcends experience. Yet truth is not void of experience. Despite the critics, Pentecostals do not base their beliefs solely on personal experience. They can also articulate their conclusions on this topic of "tongues" expositively. Regeneration can be expositionally explained, but it isn't until one has been experientially born again that the intellectual part of man can truly appreciate and comprehend the Spirit-provoked inner joy and peace of the occasion. The same can be said of the baptism with the Holy Spirit.

It's likely that my expositional explanation may not fully resound with a reader who hasn't personally experienced the gift. Nonetheless, below are some reasons why most Pentecostals conclude that *glossolalia*, or "tongues," is the initial evidence of one having received the baptism with the Holy Spirit, and the subsequent Spirit-prompted utterance of deep worship and prayer. I should add that not all Pentecostals are adamant in viewing *tongues* as the exclusive evidence. However, there is no human spiritual experience like that of being in a revival-type service where the presence of God and worship is overwhelming, where the Word of God is delivered with such a power of the Holy Spirit's anointing that it penetrates the hardest heart, where there is hardly a dry eye in the room, and where there is pure and profound worship flowing from the spirit through the lips of worshipers, which may indeed include 'tongues.' Some of you readers may have experienced this glory to some degree. Some perhaps long for what I'm describing, either because you've tasted of it long ago and your spirit bears witness to what I'm describing, or because you're thirsting for what you sense is true from God's Word but have never personally witnessed or experienced it. Others, even with exposure to the genuine, may be dismissive, and even mock (**Isaiah 28:11-12; Acts 2:13**).

Regarding the baptism with the Holy Spirit, the various accounts from the book of Acts indicate, or infer, that whenever this baptism with the Holy Spirit was given, a supernatural manifestation of some kind occurred. Acts recounts six such occurrences: The 120 disciples (**Acts 2:4**); Jewish believers (**Acts 4:31**); the Samaritans (**Acts 8:18**); Saul (**Acts 9:17**); Cornelius (**Acts 10:44**); and the Ephesians (**Acts 19:6**). Whenever that manifestation is identified by Luke (*the author of Acts*), the common manifestation denominator among them all was *tongues*. It is clearly stated as such in the case of the 120 disciples, Cornelius, and the Ephesians.

On the day of Pentecost (**Acts 2**), the 120 disciples were all in one accord and in expectation of the 'Father's Promise,' that Jesus, ten days earlier, moments before his ascension, had instructed them to tarry for (**Luke 24:49**). Suddenly, the supernatural presence of God filled the room. They were all filled with the Holy Spirit and began to speak with other tongues as the Spirit gave them utterance. They were all filled and given their individual utterance by the Spirit, but they volitionally spoke as prompted. They did not do so because the Spirit in any manner overwhelmed them by force. Regarding 'tongues,' or any other of the manifestational gifts, the individual always retains control (**1 Corinthians 14:32**), either to give way to, properly refrain, or improperly resist, the Spirit of God's promptings (**1 Corinthians 14:27-31, 39**).

In the case of the Jewish believers (**Acts 4**), we're not told whether there were some present there that had not yet received the baptism with the Holy Spirit. We do know that Peter and John, who were present, had received it, that other believers were present at that location, and that *everyone* present on that occasion was filled with the Holy Spirit. The lasting result was an empowerment of boldness to continue declaring the Gospel in the face of persecution. Pentecostal doctrine believes that there is one initial (*subsequent to regeneration*) baptism with the Holy Spirit, but there may be many refillings. At minimum, this refilling was the case for Peter and John in chapter 4.

In the case of the Samaritans (**Acts 8**), a manifestation is implied but not identified. Whatever it was, the manifestation resulting from the power of the Apostles laying hands on individuals was greatly coveted by Simon (*the "Sorcerer"*). Clearly, when the apostles laid hands on those believers, something specific and glorious took place. It could not have been salvation, because an outward manifestation of regeneration is generally not immediately discernible. Besides, as already noted, these Samaritans had already believed and had been obedient to the initial ordinance of water ('*believer's*') baptism. When comparing Scripture with Scripture, the manifestation that so caught Simon's attention must have been the great sense of visible blessing and outward joy produced by the baptism with the Holy Spirit that was accompanied by the supernatural phenomenon of tongues worship.

In the case of Saul (**Acts 9**), no mention at all is made of any supernatural manifestation other than the miraculous restoration of Saul's sight. However, later Paul (*after conversion, Saul's name was changed to Paul*), confessed this, "*I thank my God, I speak with tongues more than ye all*" (**1 Corinthians 14:18**). It can be quite safely concluded from the other passages on this subject that Paul's first tongues experience was likely at the moment he was filled, or baptized, with the Holy Spirit through the laying on of hands by Ananias.

In the (**Acts 10**) case of the large expectant group of non-Jewish people waiting for Peter at Cornelius' house (**Acts 10:24-27, 34-46**), there was no solicitation, no altar call, and no laying on of hands. While Peter was preaching, the Spirit simply was "*poured out*" and "*fell on*" all those who heard (*believed*) the Word. The convincing proof for Peter and the Jews being, that they heard these Gentiles "*speak with tongues and magnify God*"!

In the Ephesians' case of **Acts 19** (**vss. 1-7**), when these already baptized (and after they were taught correctly, re-water baptized) believers thereafter had Paul lay his hands on them, the Holy Spirit "*came on*" them, and they "*spake with tongues and prophesied*"!

In the face of the above direct and circumstantial Scriptural evidence, the Pentecostal will argue it can be legitimately concluded that the common denominator of the initial outward evidence of having received the baptism with the Holy Spirit is 'glossolalia;' i.e., Spirit-prompted tongues. It certainly was the convincing factor for Peter and the Jews who accompanied him to the house of Cornelius (**Acts 10:45-46**)![11] It was also the conclusive and convincing evidence that Peter presented upon his return to the contentious and suspicious Christian leaders of Jewish descent in Jerusalem (**Acts 11:15-18**).[12] This 'tongues evidence' can be strongly inferred because it was the proof accepted by the original Jerusalem Church leaders! Yet today not all are dogmatic in this.

Another observation by non-Pentecostals that casts doubt for them on the legitimacy of tongues as a reoccurring phenomenon beyond the initial upper room descendance of the Spirit at Pentecost, is the raising of the question as to why tongues should be an expected reoccurring phenomenon while there is no record of a sound from heaven like a rushing might wind, or tongues of fire, ever reoccurring. This is a legitimate question, but the Pentecostal will explain that the wind and fire were single-event signs of the *giving* or *coming* of the Spirit. Tongues is the reoccurring sign of one having *received* the baptism with the Spirit. In reference to the wind and fire question, Assemblies of God theologians suggest the wind was a commonly recognized symbol for the Holy Spirit, while the fire was a symbol of acceptance, as of a sacrifice, as foretold by John the Baptist when he said, "*He (Jesus) shall baptize you with the Holy Ghost and with fire,*" (**Luke 3:16**). Of the wind and fire, they conclude, "All this remarkable manifestation must have spoken loudly to the 120 that the Holy Spirit was now given."[13]

Pentecostal evangelist Jimmy Swaggart adds this observation; "The sound of the rushing, mighty wind, tongues of fire, and speaking in tongues are mentioned collectively only in this one single passage (**Acts 2:1-4**); however, tongues are mentioned and discussed some 22 times in the Word of God."[14] None the less, Cessationist seminary professor Luis C. Ruiz argues in chapter 2 of his exegesis of Spirit and water baptism, entitled, *The Battle for Biblical Baptism*, (The Old Paths Publications, 2020), that the "*baptism with the Holy Ghost, and with fire*" (**Matthew 3:11**) is referring to two baptisms; the first a blessing, but the second (*fire*) a damnation judgment to flee from! Ruiz condemns coupling the two together as both being blessings, calling that union (*on page 26 of his book*), an "*abominable teaching.*"

I would be remiss if in this subsection on "tongues evidence" I neglected to again touch on the Pentecostal response to the concept of *Cessationism*. As a reminder, Cessationists are those who only historically accept the tongues phenomena (generally limited to the ability to speak in previously unlearned foreign languages, as in **Acts 2**). They adamantly insist that four so-called 'sign' gifts, of the nine listed in **1 Corinthians 12:8-10**, were in existence solely during the First Century, and were limited to the signification or authentication of the original Apostles. The remaining five manifestation gifts are reinterpreted to be non-miraculous operations. Cessationsist Leslie B. Flynn says; "Four gifts … qualify as *sign* gifts … The gifts of miracles, healing and tongues (*and interpretation*) all possessed sign value in apostolic times."[15] The Cessationists' conclusion from **1 Corinthians 13:8-12**[16] is that after the first century, or upon the completed canon of New Testament scripture, tongues ceased, or became extinct in the New Testament church. Charles C. Ryrie argues the point this way:

"There are positive indications in verse 8 that tongues would cease before prophecies and knowledge. Of prophecies (the oral communication of God's truth before the books of the canon were written) and knowledge (the special understanding of these prophecies) it is written that they shall be done away (*katargeo*, 'rendered inoperative'). Of tongues it is said that they shall cease (*pauo*). Furthermore, the verb 'done away' used in connection with prophecies and knowledge is in the passive voice, indicating that someone (God) shall make them inoperative. The verb 'cease' used in connection with tongues is middle voice, indicating that they would die out of their own accord."[17]

But Howard M. Ervin, a former Baptist minister who later became a Pentecostal scholar, is very direct in addressing the Cessationsists' interpretation of **1 Corinthians 13:8-12**. Ervin quite pointedly attributes Paul's intent, not to the completed canon of New Testament scripture, but to the Second Coming *Parousia* (Christ's second-coming appearance and abiding). He states:

"Expediency and / or apologetic intent have led some to define 'that which is perfect' as the completed canon of Scripture. In support of this view, the charisms of 'prophecy' and 'knowledge' are restricted in operation to revelatory gifts given for the sole purpose of communicating the New Testament revelation.

However, the whole thesis is devastated by the argument *reductio ad absurdum*. A simple paraphrase of Paul's words will serve to illustrate this contention, e.g.: 'Now,' wrote Paul, 'I know in part; but then (when the canon of the New Testament is completed) shall I know fully even as also I was fully known.' The absurdity of this is readily apparent. The apostle was dead, martyred, before the corpus of the New Testament was completed. By way of contrast, he spoke specifically of himself, and of his own expectations when he said, 'then shall I know.' He anticipated the time when his own partial knowledge - 'seen in a mirror dimly' - would be completed. Clearly, he was looking forward to the second coming of our Lord and Savior Jesus Christ when he penned these words, at which time, his own fragmentary knowledge would be completed ... The apostolic age began with miraculous signs and wonders. After the day of Pentecost, 'tongues' were followed in rapid succession by all, and more, of the charisms of the Holy Spirit enumerated in **1 Corinthians 12-14**. And it is the plain testimony of Scripture that these supernatural manifestations of the Holy Spirit were to continue throughout the whole of the Church age, terminating only at the second advent of our Lord Jesus Christ."[18]

More can be said of how the baptism with the Holy Spirit was typified in the Old Testament; i.e., by paralleling the dedication of the Temple (**2 Chronicles 5:11-14**) with the empowerment of the infant New Testament church (**Acts 2**). In both; manifestations of 'shekinah glory' at the Temple dedication, and tongues, wind and fire at the Pentecost New Testament Church launch, it was the strong unity in worship that made way for the Spirit to move. Note also how this baptism with the Spirit was promised in the Gospels by both John the Baptist and Jesus Christ, and how it was referred to in the Epistles and experienced by various churches. Despite historical gaps, such as in the "Dark Ages," when not only glossolalia was dormant in the Church, but many other fundamental Christian truths as well. Yet "tongues" has consistently reoccurred as the common phenomena associated with receiving the *subsequent* baptism with the Holy Spirit.

The mature Pentecostal does not rely on personal experience alone. Admittedly, theological truth cannot be based on personal experiences. As the Apostle Peter, referring to his amazing experience of witnessing Christ's transfiguration understood (**Matthew 17:2; 2 Peter 1:18-19**), God's Word is far superior to all genuine spiritual experiences! But God's Word initiates and substantiates the justification for the doctrinal positions taken on the contemporary relevancy of the baptism with the Holy Spirit, and its association with the phenomena of tongues. However, this 'secondary' area of theology should not be a cause for division among Christians, because it must be understood that it is not in competition to the essential soteriological doctrine of the regenerating Spirit baptism unto salvation.

B. Qualifications for the Baptism with the Holy Spirit

We've touched on this topic previously, so it can be briefly restated here. For the Pentecostal, the baptism with the Holy Spirit is not the initial regenerational Spirit baptism unto salvation. It a subsequent-to-salvation gift of God to empower his Church. According to Jesus' announcement of the coming Comforter in **John 14:16-17**,[19] the (unbelieving) world cannot receive Him. Therefore, the honest Bible student concludes that the baptism with the Holy Spirit is a separate and subsequent event intended for the already redeemed of God. The 'time lapse' from Spirit-regenerational belief that produces salvation, to the baptism 'filling' *with* the Spirit, can be either nearly simultaneous (*as it was with the conversion and immediate subsequent filling of Cornelius' household of* **Acts 10**), or after an unspecified period of time (*as with the Samaritan and Ephesian converts of* **Acts 8** and **19**). Here is the foundation for this belief:

It is commonly held that the first Pentecost, subsequent to the Resurrection and ten days after the ascension of Jesus Christ, when the empowering Holy Spirit initially descended on the 120 in the Jerusalem upper room (**Acts 1-2** *[2:1-4]*), was the "birth" of the New Testament Church. This is a necessary position for the non-Pentecostal who insists 'tongues' was limited to the birth and early establishment of the Church, as the beginning act of the Great Commission's Gospel proclamation. This interpretation also attempts to shore up the belief that the Spirit's descent at Pentecost was the initial New Testament regenerational baptism unto salvation, in transition from the Old Testament economy.

However, as was previously established, the thoughtful and honest Bible scholar will concede that it was on the evening of Resurrection Day, "when He (*the resurrected, pre-ascended, pre-glorified Jesus*) breathed on *them*, and said unto them, "*Receive ye the Holy Ghost*" (**John 20:22**), that the threshold from the Old Testament to the New was crossed. In fact, according to Jesus' previous words of **John 14:17**, the Holy Spirit was already dwelling *with* them, but was soon to be *in* them. The disciples, at the very moment that Jesus breathed on them to receive the Holy Spirit *in* them, became the first New Testament "born-again" regenerated believers. The resurrected Jesus had at this time not yet ascended, he was not yet glorified, and he had not yet been at the Father's right hand to receive the 'Father's Promise' (**Acts 2:33**[20]). The resurrected Jesus was fully able to give eternal life, but not yet able to give the Father's Promise because He had not yet ascended to receive it from the Father. Therefore, it bears repeating that the 'breathing' could not have been the fulfillment of the coming promised Comforter, and Pentecost could not have been the initial spiritual regeneration experience. Jesus' breathing placed the Spirit *in* them, while the Holy Spirit's empowering came *upon* them!

This issue is further clarified by placing the events on a Biblical timeline. Earlier, Jesus had declared; "*If any man thirst, let him come unto me and drink. He that believeth on me, as the scripture hath said, out of his belly shall flow rivers of living water,*" (**John 7:37b-38**). John's comment on Jesus' declaration was, "(*But this spake he of the Spirit, which they that believe on him should receive: for the Holy Ghost was not yet given; because that Jesus was not yet glorified*)" (**John 7:39**). Therefore, this giving and overflowing of the Holy Spirit could not have been the breathing impartation because when Jesus breathed on the disciples, he had not yet ascended and been glorified. Jesus was here speaking of the post-ascension initial sending of the Spirit at Pentecost, and the continuing Father's Promise for the Church Age.

Howard Ervin states the point this way:

"...others have equated the outpouring of the Holy Spirit upon the Church at Pentecost with the beginning of the new covenant. It is this assumption that underlies the oft-repeated cliché, 'Pentecost is the birthday of the Church.' This, however, is tantamount to saying that the disciples of Jesus were born again by the descent of the Holy Spirit on that day. This in turn has led to the self-defeating assumption that at conversion all believers are filled automatically with the Spirit."[21]

Ervin goes on to distinguish the two events (pre-ascended breathing, and post-ascended sending of the Spirit) in this manner:

"The Paschal bestowal of the Holy Spirit was ontological; it involved a change of nature, a new birth. The sending of the Spirit upon the disciples at Pentecost was functional, i.e., empowerment for service."[22]

The Biblical conclusion is that upon salvation, the believer receives the regenerating Holy Spirit within him. This was initiated at Jesus' 'breathing' occasion (**John 20:22**) on the evening of Resurrection Day, which was the event marking the completion of Jesus' atoning work. On that occasion, before Jesus breathed on the ten Apostles (*Judas Iscariot was dead and not yet replaced, and Thomas apparently had stepped out,* **John 20:24**), and whoever else may have been present (i.e., *at minimum Cleopas and his companion,* **Luke 24:18,33**), He gave them a hint of the Great Commission, saying, "*as my Father hath sent me, even so send I you,*" (**John 20:21**). Then, 40 days later, on Ascension Day, Jesus gave them more detailed instructions concerning the Great Commission to be carried out to all nations, but instructed them not to go anywhere until they became empowered with the 'Father's Promise' to fulfil that mandate (**Matthew 28:19-20; Luke 24:49**). Therefore, the baptism with the Holy Spirit is subsequent to the new birth, and for the empowerment of regenerated believers. The empowering Comforter could not be sent until after Jesus "went away" (**John 16:7**),[23] or ascended, so that He could be glorified and receive the Church giftings from the Father.

Again, at Pentecost, the Apostle Peter announced the Spirit's coming as the fulfillment of the "Father's promise" (**Acts 2:33**). Just prior to the ascension, the disciples had been commanded by Jesus not to, "*depart from Jerusalem, but wait for the promise of the Father,*"

(**Acts 1:4b-5**). In Luke's gospel, Jesus had been quoted as follows: "*And, behold, I send the promise of my Father upon you: but tarry ye in the city of Jerusalem, until ye be endued with power from on high,*" (**Luke 24:49**). The Apostle John had already identified the Father's promise as being the Comforter, (**John 14:16-17**; and **16:7**). These instructions were given to the disciples 40 days *after* Jesus had breathed on them to receive the Holy Spirit, and just *prior* to the ascension. I've repeatedly emphasized this truth to establish that the 'Father's Promise' of the Spirit's empowerment is not universal, but *'limited'* and available to only those who've already been born again.

Understanding this concept is key to clarifying of the Calvinist's misapplied "*limited atonement*" position, which is the central one of the five tenets of Calvinism. The Spirit baptism of salvation is for regeneration of the human spirit. All who hear the good news have equal opportunity to receive this gift. Regeneration unto salvation is offered to "*whosoever will,*" (**John 3:15-16**; **Revelation 22:17**). But the offer of Spirit empowerment is restricted, or *limited* to those who are called to Christ and have responded to salvation. It is exclusively for the soul-empowerment of the believer who has already experienced a regenerated spirit.

C. The Trinity's Work in Spiritual Giftings

As it is with salvation, in that it is an act of grace from the Father made available only as result of the accomplished work of the Son and effected in the lives of men by the regenerating action of the Spirit, so are the baptism with the Holy Spirit and spiritual giftings to the Church a work of the Trinity.

1) The Godhead Source

It is from the ***Father*** that the outflow of all blessings originate (**James 1:17**). It is the ***Son*** who has bridged the previously impassable chasm between the one true holy God and sinful man. It is the ***Holy Spirit*** who is the Agent applying the blessings to men. The Apostle Paul said, "*Blessed be the God and Father of our Lord Jesus Christ, who hath blessed us with all spiritual blessings in heavenly places in Christ,*" (**Ephesians 1:3**). It is the three divine Persons of our One triune God who is at work in the giftings. *"Diversities of gifts"* are applied by the same <u>Spirit</u>, the *"differences of administrations"* by the same <u>Lord</u>, and *"diversities of operations"* by the same <u>God</u> that is at work in all (**1 Corinthians 12:4-6**).

As previously stated, the baptism *with* the Holy Spirit is the 'Promise of the **Father**' to believers. It is the **Son** who upon his ascension and glorification received the gift from the Father for Jesus' baptismal outpouring to believers. It is the **Holy Spirit** who manifests the gift as He fills, comforts, edifies, enables, equips and empowers the receiving saints. Like salvation, all proceeds <u>from the Father</u>, <u>through the Son</u> (**Matthew 11:27**; **John 10:28, 17:2**), <u>by the Spirit</u>. In salvation it is the Holy Spirit who effectuates the new birth by placing the believer into the Body of Christ. In the baptism *with* the Holy Spirit, it is Jesus who baptizes and the Holy Spirit who ministers its effects.

On the question of *glossolalia* believed by many to be the manifested evidence of receiving the baptism with the Holy Spirit, the Scriptures tell us that, *"…they were all filled with the Holy Ghost, and began to speak with other tongues, as the Spirit gave them utterance,"* (**Acts 2:4**). It is the Holy Spirit that in His filling, urges and inspires the utterance. On the day of Pentecost, the Apostle Peter explained to the curious crowd that the ascended Jesus, *"…being by the right hand of God exalted, and having received of the Father the promise of the Holy Ghost, he hath shed forth this, which ye now see and hear,"* (**Acts 2:33**).

The genuine tongues utterance cannot originate and be formulated in man's mind. It must originate from the Spirit of God so that the speaking is not a learned, rehearsed, or thought-out discourse, but rather a spontaneous utterance urged on from within the individual as prompted by the Spirit's strong presence. The practice by some of teaching individuals to speak with tongues is folly. It renders the manufactured utterance as counterfeit, phony, and void of power. The presence of God in a congregational meeting of believers, or in a believer's heart, cannot be manufactured. This is why the disciples were instructed to *"tarry ye in the city of Jerusalem"* (**Luke 24:49b**) and *"wait for the promise of the Father"* (**Acts 1:4b**). They were to wait there for the moving of the Spirit. Meanwhile Jesus, *"having received of the Father the promise of the Holy Ghost"* (**Acts 2:33**), then sent the same down to the obedient, unified, awaiting disciples. Once the Spirit came and did his work of infilling, the disciples "*began to speak with other tongues, as the Spirit gave them utterance,*" (**Acts 2:4b**).

2) The Godhead Attributes

The Holy Spirit, the third Person of the Godhead, is God. As such, He possesses all of the attributes of personality and all the divine attributes, to include omnipotence and omnipresence. The Spirit-regenerated believer becomes the temple of the Holy Spirit (**1 Corinthians 6:19**). But this certainly does not mean that God the Holy Spirit's presence is restricted within the physical bodies of believers! This idea is generally a Baptistic position based on an incomplete interpretation of **Matthew 18:20**; "*For where two or three are gathered together in my name, there am I in the midst of them.*" The Baptistic view states that when believers meet, the Holy Spirit's presence is ushered in by the attendees who 'bring Him in with them.'

This Baptistic interpretation of **Matthew 18:20** is a necessary one to downplay and repress what might be an 'uncomfortable' moving of the Spirit that might cause 'odd' behaviors in a worship service. But it is actually also necessary as a support to most Baptists' eschatological position of pre-tribulation rapturism! Pre-tribulationism is embraced by many evangelicals, to include most Baptists and Pentecostals, and it places the Church's Rapture at the beginning of the "70th Week" (**Daniel 9:27**), that they believe takes place at **Revelation 4:1**. If, as they say, the Holy Spirit is the "restrainer" holding back the Antichrist (**2 Thessalonians 2:7-8**), then the Antichrist is unleashed when the Church ('housing' the Holy Spirit), is removed from the earth at the Rapture. However, there is solid Biblical evidence the 'restrainer' is not the Holy Spirit, but rather, the archangel Michael (**Daniel 10:21b**; **12:1**). Clearly, the Rapture is described taking place at **Revelation 7:9** (which coincides with Jesus' Olivet Discourse of **Matthew 24:31**), and it has nothing to do with the Holy Spirit being '*removed*' …a discussion for another day. The point to be made here is that the Holy Spirit is God. His presence transcends and is not limited to, nor confined within, the body of the Church. His movements are not restricted by us (**John 3:8**). The only thing that limits the working of the Holy Spirit on man, is man's resistance (**Acts 7:51**), and unbelief (**Matthew 13:58**). In both Old and

New Testament times, when believers met together, it was faith and unity of worship that invited the Holy Spirit's manifested presence (**2 Chronicles 5:13; Acts 2:1-4, 4:31-32**).

3) The Godhead Gifts

It must also be stated here that the various gifts of the Spirit to the Church (only one of which is 'tongues'), are also all given by grace through the Spirit. Generally speaking, many evangelicals may agree with Baptist Pastor Leslie B. Flynn's assessment that there are *nineteen* gifts of the Holy Spirit mentioned in the New Testament.[24] He cites eighteen enumerated in three passages of scripture (**Romans 12:6-8; 1 Corinthians 12:8-10**; and **Ephesians 4:11**).[25] And a nineteenth gift of "hospitality" mentioned by the Apostle Peter (**1 Peter 4:9-10**).[26] These nineteen gifts are classified by Flynn into three groups; *speaking* gifts, *serving* gifts, and *signifying* gifts. He lists the eight <u>speaking</u> gifts as: *Apostleship, prophecy, evangelism, pastoring, teaching, exhorting, word of wisdom,* and *word of knowledge.* The seven <u>serving</u> gifts as: *Ministration (helps), hospitality, giving, government (ruling), showing mercy, faith,* and *discernment.* With four being considered <u>signifying</u> gifts: *tongues, interpretation (of tongues), miracles,* and *healing.* But Baptists and Pentecostals tend to disagree with how Flynn lumps together and defines these gifts, and how they operate in the Church.

Consider this analogy: A bowl of fruit may contain three categories of fruit within it – say, grapes, apples, and citrus fruit. The same bowl may also contain various kinds of grapes (red, green, black, purple, seeded, seedless…etc); various kinds of apples (Granny, Gala, Fuji, Honeycrisp, Empire… etc); and various kinds of citrus fruit (oranges, tangerines, limes, lemons, grapefruit… etc). Similarly, we must understand the Bible teaches us that, "*there are diversities of gifts,*" "*differences of administrations,*" and "*diversities of operations,*" but the same Spirit, same Lord, and the same God that works in all of them (**1 Corinthians 12:4-6**).

Therefore, we find that there are three categories of spiritual gifts, with various sub-types: The <u>**seven** *Motivational* Gifts</u> of the <u>Father</u> listed in **Romans 12:6-8** (prophecy, ministry, teaching, exhortation, giving, ruling *[or 'administration']*, mercy, plus an 8th 'hospitality,' required for pastors *[1 Pet. 4:9-10 / 1 Tim. 3:2]*); the **five _Ministry_ Gifts** of <u>Christ</u> listed in **Ephesians 4:11** (apostles, prophets, evangelists, pastors/teachers); and the **nine _Manifestational_** <u>Gifts</u> of the <u>Spirit</u> as listed in **1 Corinthians 12:7-10** (word of wisdom, word of knowledge, faith, gifts of healing(s), working of miracles, prophecy, discerning of spirits, divers kinds of tongues, and interpretation of tongues).

The <u>motivational gifts</u> are '*natural*' God-given aptitudes, inclinations, or motivating endowments given to all, saved and unsaved, but emerge to be exercised by believers within the Church. The <u>ministry gifts</u> are '*calling*' positions of service within the Church. The <u>manifestational gifts</u> operate '*supernaturally*' in saved individuals, who God wills, as prompted by the Holy Spirit. While every gift originates from the Father (**James 1:17**), we see the full Godhead is engaged! The three categories of gifts are all Spirit-driven and dispensed by *grace* (Motivational - **Romans 12:6**; Ministry – **Ephesians 4:7**; and Manifestational – **1 Corinthians 1:4-5**). Some of these varying gifts that Flynn lumps together, are called by the same term, even though they're listed in different categories. While the gifts from the various categories can be interrelated, they have differing functions and purposes within the Body of Christ. For example, the gift of 'motivational' prophecy (*humanly driven*) is not identical in its exercise and function as the gift of 'manifestational' prophecy (*supernaturally driven forth & fore-telling*).

Furthermore, in **1 Corinthians 12:28**, the Holy Spirit inspired the Apostle Paul to record the prioritization of the various categories and sub-types of gifts in their order of importance; "*And God hath set* [firmly placed] *some in the Church* [not just the 1st C. Church] *first apostles* [visionaries, mission and church planting overseers], *secondarily prophets* [words of knowledge, words of wisdom, discernment of spirits], *thirdly teachers* [pastor-teachers, evangelists], *after that miracles, then gifts of healings, helps* [mercy, giving, hospitality], *governments* [ruling/administration], *divers kinds of tongues* [and interpretation of tongues]." It does well to repeat that the three categories of gifts are given by <u>grace</u>, not by merit or for performance-rewards (*motivation* – **Rom. 12:6**; *ministry* – **Eph. 4:7**; and *manifestation* – **1 Cor. 1:4-5**). God beautifully emphasized this point by giving an over-abundance of giftings to the Corinthian church that we might consider the 'least worthy.' Perhaps if we were the administrators of the spiritual gifts, we might have granted the lion's share of gifts to the more meritoriously *"noble"* Bereans (**Acts 17:10-11**).

Another observation that can be made concerning the nine manifestational spiritual gifts, enumerated by the Apostle Paul in **1 Corinthians 12:8-10**, is that they are commonly divided by most Pentecostals into three sub-categories. Jimmy Swaggart's analysis of this is as follows:

> "Three of the gifts (the *"word of wisdom,"* the *"word of knowledge,"* and the *"discerning of spirits"*) are revelation gifts (they reveal something). The second group (*"faith," "healing[s],"* and *"working of miracles"*) do something. And the last category (*"prophecy," "tongues,"* and *"interpretation of tongues"*) say something."²⁷

Finally, we can also observe that in God's method of divine triangulation, the five-fold Ministry Gifts to the church catalogued in **Ephesians 4:11** (apostles, prophets, evangelists, pastors, teachers), are clearly stated to be for a three-fold purpose: **1)** *"For the perfecting of the saints"*; **2)** *"for the work of the ministry,"* and **3)** *"for the edifying of the body of Christ,"* (**Ephesians 4:12**). Similarly, the manifestational gift of prophecy is for a three-fold purpose: **1)** to edify; **2)** exhort; and **3)** comfort (**1 Corinthians 14:3**).

Note that the primary emphasis of these gifts is to disciple, build up, instruct, mature, the body of believers! The focus of the giftings is not for the recruitment of new converts as the Church's number-one goal. A healthy and mature church will organically reproduce itself. New converts will be attracted and added if there is spiritual life in the Church. When the church is alive and well, spiritually hungry souls will be drawn, member believers will grow in their faith and they will then confidently and excitedly invite their unconverted friends without fear of embarrassment.

Sadly, there are many Pentecostals and Charismatics who, like the Corinthians, are in dire need Biblical instruction and guidelines in the exercise of these spiritual gifts. Also sadly, there are many 'main-line' Christians who sincerely believe they are following the truth of the Bible with the illumination of the Spirit, but will typically reject or misinterpret the manifestation gifts, and also omit the first two of the five ministry gifts (*apostles* and *prophets*) as not being relevant for today. To them, 'apostles' no longer exist, and 'prophets' as foretellers have been retired. In rightly rejecting the Roman Catholic model of apostolic succession, they fail to acknowledge that others besides the original twelve were regarded as 'apostles' (*example: clearly Paul, but also Barnabas* – **Acts 14:4, 14**). **Revelation 2:2** strongly suggests that there were true and false apostles beyond the original twelve!

Additionally, the "prophet" gift is in all cases reinterpreted by Cessationists in the 'motivational-gift' sense, to mean anyone (*any preacher or witnessing lay person*) who is in some way gifted or trained to proclaim God's Word, but never as a revealer or 'foreteller.' Unfortunately, this cessationist position originates more from a tradition of rejecting what one doesn't understand or want to believe concerning all the various gifts of the Spirit to the Church, than it is on the plain 'face-value' teaching of the Bible. Often this rejection is based on the exegetical errors by Cessationists, as well as by the poor example and excesses of Corinthian-like unlearned Pentecostals and Charismatics.

For example, we must distinguish the Old Testament *prophet* from the New Testament manifestational *gift of prophecy*. The Scriptures are clear that Old Testament prophets (*when the full canon of the written Word was yet incomplete*) were judged differently than how post-canon New Testament prophets ought to be judged. In the Old Testament, an erring prophet who misdirected people from the LORD, was worthy of death (**Deuteronomy 13:1-5; 18:20-22**). This was true even if their prophecy appeared authenticated by their prophesied sign or wonder coming to pass! Not so in the New Testament, where believers are cautioned not to believe every spirit, but rather to "*try the spirits whether they are of God*" (**1 John 4:1-3**). John warns, "*Let no man deceive you*" (**1 John 3:7**). During the end-time 'Great Tribulation' there shall be false 'christs' and prophets performing great signs and wonders that would appear sufficiently credible to, if possible, deceive and seduce even the elect! (**Matthew 24:24; Mark 13:22**). Yet, during that time, the manifestational 'Word of Wisdom' gift will be critical (**Mark 13:11; Luke 21:13-15**)! There is a significant difference in how God's people were taught to deal with false Old Testament prophets and how we are to judge New Testament gifts of prophecy.

While everything is to be done in decency and order, prophecy ought to be a desired operating gift and tongues are not to be forbidden (**1 Corinthians 14:39-40**). The validity of a prophet's proclamation is to be examined and judged by the standard of the completed Word of God (**1 Corinthians 14:29**). God's Word is infinitely superior and *"more sure"* than any genuine, even extraordinary, manifestation (**2 Peter 1:19-21**)! Prophecies are not to be despised, but rather proven without discarding that which is good (**1 Thessalonians 5:19-21**). Unlike the Old Testament (**Deuteronomy 13:5** & **18:20**), there is no physical death penalty for the erring New Testament prophet. But those identified as divisive or misleading false-prophets are to be marked as such and avoided (**Romans 16:17**).

Untangling, in this chapter, the obscurities of the "Baptism *with* the Holy Spirit," we've affirmed that every good and perfect gift originates from God the Father (**James 1:17**), and that the 'motivational' gifts listed in **Romans 12:6-8** are apportioned to *every* person by the Father. However, the dissemination of the 'ministry' gifts (**Ephesians 4:11**) was delegated to the Son (**Ephesians 4:7**). Likewise, the dispensing of the 'manifestational' gifts was delegated to the Holy Spirit. Like the Son, the Holy Spirit is always in sync with the mind of the Father (**Romans 8:27**), and therefore has the authority to dispense these gifts severally as He wills (**1 Corinthians 12:11**). Having established that, and that the *baptizer* of the 'baptism *with* the Holy Spirit' is Christ (**Mark 1:8; Acts 1:5, 11:16**), which is for the purpose of empowering His believers for the Church to minister effectively (**Acts 1:8**), and for which He had to first ascend (**John 16:7**), we may safely categorize the Baptism with the Holy Spirit as perhaps the first of the *Ministry Gifts* of Christ. But unlike the other the Ministry Gifts listed in **Ephesians 4:11**, which are apportioned discriminately and individually, *"and he gave some... and some... and some... and some,"* it appears that *every* believer in Christ is eligible to receive this empowering Baptism with the Holy Spirit (**Acts 2:16-18, 33, 39**). The believer must volitionally receive this gift that will be of great benefit, both to himself and, by consequence, to the broader Body of Christ. On the Day of Pentecost, the Spirit filled and gave the praying believers the utterance, but they had to speak the utterance forth by faith (**Acts 2:4**). While verses **37-41** of **Acts 2** transition the *"gift of the Holy Ghost"* to salvation (as in **1 Corinthians 12:13**), the origin of the discussion in this chapter was with reference to the 'baptism *with* the Holy Spirit.' Peter explained the 'Promise of the Father,' and how it was received by Christ from the Father and then dispensed for the empowerment of His Church. But Peter then properly shifted to preaching the central gospel message of Christ, and the promise of eternal salvation for all who believe in Christ as Savior, and submit themselves to God by faith in repentance and obedience.

One final observation in this chapter regarding God's purposes for "tongues." In **Genesis 11:1-9**, God used 'tongues' to scatter *ungodly* people throughout the world, who were bent on their own methods and object(s) of worship. In **Acts 2:1-13**, God used 'tongues' to gather *believing* people, and to signify to the world that the Gospel message of redemption (i.e., the "*wonderful works of God*," verse 11), was now intended for the benefit of all peoples throughout the world! Would to God, He would in some way use this book to help bring understanding and unity among believers of precious like-faith!

CHAPTER NINE ENDNOTES

[1] MacArthur, 188.

[2] *"I indeed have baptized you with water: but he shall baptize you with the Holy Ghost,"* (**Mark 1:8**); *"For John truly baptized with water; but ye shall be baptized with the Holy Ghost not many days hence,"* (**Acts 1:5**); *"Then remembered I the word of the Lord, how that he said, John indeed baptized with water; but ye shall be baptized with the Holy Ghost,"* (**Acts 11:16**).

[3] James Strong, *Strong's Greek Dictionary of the New Testament*, (Nashville: Crusade Bible Publishers), 68.

[4] *"For by one Spirit are we all baptized into one body..."* (**1 Corinthians 12:13a**).

[5] *"Go ye therefore, and teach all nations, baptizing them in the name of the Father, and of the Son, and of the Holy Ghost,"* (**Matthew 28:20**).

[6] *"I indeed baptize you with water unto repentance: but he that cometh after me is mightier than I, whose shoes I am not worthy to bear: he shall baptize you with the Holy Ghost, and with fire,"* (**Matthew 3:11**); *"I have need to be baptized of thee,"* (**Matthew 3:14b**).

[7] *"And I will pray the Father, and he shall give you another Comforter, that he may abide with you forever; Even the Spirit of Truth; whom the world cannot receive, because it seeth him not, neither knoweth him: but ye know him; for he dwelleth with you, and shall be in you,"* (**John 14:16-17**).

[8] *"Nevertheless I tell you the truth; It is expedient for you that I go away: for if I go not away, the Comforter will not come unto you; but if I depart, I will send him unto you,"* (**John 16:7**).

[9] Hank Hanegraaff, *Counterfeit Revival*, (Dallas: Word Publishing, 1997), 95.

[10] Hanegraaff, 157.

[11] *"And they of the circumcision which believed were astonished, as many as came with Peter, because that on the Gentiles also was poured out the gift of the Holy Ghost. For they heard them speak with tongues, and magnify God,"* (**Acts 10:45-46a**).

[12] *"And as I began to speak, the Holy Ghost fell on them, as on us at the beginning. Then remembered I the word of the Lord, how that he said, John indeed baptized with water; but ye shall be baptized with the Holy Ghost. Forasmuch then as God gave them the like gift as he did unto us, who believed on the Lord Jesus Christ; what was I that I could withstand God? When they heard these things, they held their peace, and glorified God, saying, Then hath God also to the Gentiles granted repentance unto life,"* (**Acts 11:15-18**).

[13] Robert L. Brandt and Zenas J. Bicket, *The Spirit Helps Us Pray: A Biblical Theology of Prayer*, (Springfield, MO: Logion Press, 1997), 236.

[14] Jimmy Swaggart, *Questions & Answers*, (Baton Rouge, LA: Jimmy Swaggart Ministries, 1985), 181.

[15] Leslie B. Flynn, *19 Gifts of the Spirit*, (Wheaton: Victor Books, 1994), 39.

[16] *"Charity never faileth: but whether there be prophecies, they shall fail; whether there be tongues, they shall cease; whether there be knowledge, it shall vanish away. For we know in part, and we prophesy in part. But when that which is perfect is come, then that which is in part shall be done away. When I was a child, I spake as a child, I understood as a child, I thought as a child: but when I became a man, I put away childish things. For now we see through a glass darkly; but then face to face: now I know in part; but then shall I know even as also I am known,"* (**1 Corinthians 13:8-12**).

[17] Charles C. Ryrie, *The Holy Spirit*, (Chicago: Moody Press, 1965), 91-92.

[18] Howard M. Ervin, *Spirit Baptism*, (Peabody, MA: Hendrickson Publishers, 1987), 176.

[19] *"And I will pray the Father, and he shall give you another Comforter, that he may abide with you forever; Even the Spirit of truth; whom the world cannot receive, because it seeth him not, neither knoweth him: but ye shall know him; for he dwelleth with you, and shall be in you,"* (**John 14:16-17**).

[20] *"Therefore being by the right hand of God exalted, and having received of the Father the promise of the Holy Ghost, he hath shed forth this, which ye now see and hear,"* (**Acts 2:33**).

[21] Ervin, *Spirit Baptism*, 15.

[22] Ervin, 20.

[23] *"Nevertheless I tell you the truth; It is expedient for you that I go away; for if I go not away, the Comforter will not come unto you; but if I depart, I will send him unto you,"* (**John 16:7**).

[24] Flynn, 39.

[25] *"Having then gifts differing according to the grace that is given to us, whether prophecy, let us prophesy according to the proportion of faith; Or ministry, let us wait on our ministering: or he that teacheth, on teaching; Or he that exhorteth, on exhortation: he that giveth, let him do it with simplicity; he that ruleth, with diligence; he that showeth mercy, with cheerfulness,"* (**Romans 12:6-8**); *"For to one is given by the Spirit the word of wisdom; to another the word of knowledge by the same Spirit; To another faith by the same Spirit; to another the gifts of healing by the same Spirit; To another the working of miracles; to another prophecy; to another discerning of spirits; to another divers kinds of tongues, to another the interpretation of tongues,"* (**1 Corinthians 12:8-10**); *And God hath set some in the church, first apostles, secondarily prophets, thirdly teachers, after that miracles, then gifts of healings, helps, governments, diversities of tongues,"* (**1 Corinthians 12:28**); *"And he gave some, apostles; and some, prophets; and some, evangelists; and some, pastors and teachers,"* (**Ephesians 4:11**).

[26] *"Use hospitality one to another without grudging. As every man hath received the gift, even so minister the same one to another, as good stewards of the manifold grace of God,"* (**1 Peter 4:9-10**).

[27] Jimmy Swaggart, *Gifts of the Spirit*, (Baton Rouge, LA: Jimmy Swaggart Ministries, 1985), 7.

CONCLUSION
THE "SOUL BAPTISM"

"There is therefore now no condemnation to them which are in Christ Jesus, who walk not after the flesh, but after the Spirit."
Romans 8:1

The four themes/three blessings of the Apostle Paul's teaching in the Epistle to the Romans begins with the three-step progression, from *condemnation*, to *justification*, to *sanctification*, followed by the fourth, the eternal reward of *glorification*. The three blessings are *justification*, *sanctification*, and *glorification*. But prior to being glorified at Christ's return, our walk here on earth is one of challenge. Sinful man is under God's condemnation. Upon placing his faith in Jesus Christ and His completed work, man is redeemed through regeneration of his human spirit by the Holy Spirit, and is thereby divinely justified and positionally sanctified. The subsequent process of sanctification is accomplished in man's soul by God, but with human cooperation through faith, obedience, and discipline in the Christian life. The question arises as to how much reliance is one to have on God and how much responsibility does one bear in the process?

Throughout the centuries spanning the Church Age, doctrinal chasms developed over differing ideas of where the balance is between God's sovereignty and man's free will, and whether our salvation is secure or vulnerable to loss. And, in the last century, renewed division has re-emerged over differing ideas of how much, if any, miraculous intervention the Holy Spirit continues into the 'post-canon' New Testament Church. The focus of *Soul Baptism* has been to examine God's triune essence and His three-dimensional approach to creation, His interaction with mankind, and salvation. The goal has been to bridge doctrinal chasms through the understanding of this three-dimensional perspective, as can be seen in the Trinity, the three phases of salvation, the three distinct Christian 'baptisms,' and even the three categories of spiritual giftings!

The hypothesis of this book has been that God's ingenious threefold strategy ('*divine triangulation*') is perfect and failure-proof in its ability to accomplish all of His decrees, including salvation, and that grasping this three-dimensional strategy is the key to understanding how to bridge the doctrinal chasms. Seeing the dilemma that regenerated man faces by how his walk is affected from the tugging of the Spirit to do right, and the opposing pull of the flesh to do wrong, we concluded that the battlefield for this inner conflict is found in the realm of trichotomous man's soul. Therefore, it is the 'soul' essence of regenerated man that requires divine reinforcement for him to thrive spiritually. Grasping this truth provides opportunity more unity in the Body of Christ. Rejecting it leaves intact the confusion and divisions we've endured for much too long. The body of Christ can't afford schisms in these end-times. Paul said, "*And knowing the time, that now it is high time to awake out of sleep: for now is our salvation nearer than when we believed*" (**Romans 13:11**). If the persecuted early Church needed spiritual giftings, how much more the latter Church that will endure much greater opposing pressure! (**Matthew 24:21-22**, *which coincides with* **Revelation 6:9-11**).

To further set the context, let's consider the three-dimensional 'Seasons' of God's communion with fallen men on the earth. In the first two verses of his opening chapter, the writer to the **Hebrews** identifies the first two seasons. Throughout the Old Testament (*first season* - **Heb. 1:1**) God the Father communicated with men primarily through *prophets*. Then at the start of the New Testament era (*second season* - **Heb. 1:2; John 3:34; 14:10, 24; 17:7; 19:30**), God spoke to men through His Son, Jesus Christ (who was God incarnate on the earth bringing us the words of the Father). But when "*finished*," both prior to his death *and* ascension, Jesus repeatedly announced another era (*third* *season*), the Church Age, where the *"Comforter"* (Holy Spirit) would be operating in the work of communicating with men on the earth (**John 14:16-17, 25-26; 15:26; 16:7-8, 13; Luke 24:49; Acts 1:8; 2:33**). The Holy Spirit's work in bringing God's truth to us was accomplished by inspiring the New Testament writers, and continues through the Spirit's giftings to men throughout the Church Age! These giftings will cease when the 'third season' terminates in conjunction with Christ's 'post-Church' Second Coming.

Even the post-Church era is unfolded to us in 'three seasons'! The rapture of the Church and the events that follow in heaven (*Marriage Supper of the Lamb, etc.*) is the *first* post-Church season (**Matthew 24:31; Revelation 7:1,9**). The Millennium, when we as a royal priesthood reign with Christ 1,000 years on the earth is the *second* post-Church season (**Revelation 20:4**). After Satan's final end in the Lake of Fire (**Revelation 20:10**) there will appear a new heaven, a new earth, and a new Jerusalem, where God dwells with men permanently (**Revelation 21:1-5**). This will be the *third* and final post-Church season.

In light of the glorious truths we've reviewed, why then is the Church so stubbornly divided and blinded by such gross lack of knowledge (**Hosea 4:6**)? Can we be reconciled through new discoveries from the eternally established treasures of His Word?

A. The "Big-3" Chasms of the Faith

1) Sovereignty vs. Free Will

Reformed Christianity champions the "Five Solas." They served to correct grave errors of Roman Catholicism and were put forth as the backbone of the Protestant Reformation that proclaimed, 'salvation is by grace, through faith' alone. The 'Five Solas' are Latin phrases the Reformers coined as follows:

1. "Sola Scriptura" = *Scripture Alone*
2. "Sola Fide" = *Faith Alone*
3. "Sola Gratia" = *Grace Alone*
4. "Solus Christus" = *Christ Alone*
5. 'Soli Deo Gloria" = *Glory To God Alone*

Over the centuries, Reformed Christians have contributed much to sound Christian orthodoxy. However, their rigidly narrow interpretation of 'Sovereignty' as it relates to their view of predestination, and as expressed in the Five Tenets of Calvinism; (specifically, the three central points of *'unconditional election,' 'limited atonement,'* and *'irresistible grace,'* and the necessary *"regeneration before faith"* argument – discussed in Chapter 5), seem to reach beyond God's intent of the Bible's Gospel message of grace through faith (**Romans 5:1-2**). Arminius countered with his *'prevenient grace'* argument. But, the concept of *"Divine Triangulation"* discussed in this book, especially as seen in the 'three baptisms' (discussed in Chapter 2) can shed light on how the Reformers' views through the Word can be reconciled with the views of other evangelical Christians:

- Having equipped every man with a sufficient measure of faith, God offers salvation to *"whosoever will."* But man must *willingly* come on *God's terms,* that is, by the exercise of his faith (**Hebrews 11:6**). God's eternally perfect sovereignty is not hampered nor threatened by the free exercise of man's will. God does not need to diminish man's free will in order to retain His uncompromised sovereignty. A just God does not judge man for what he's incapable of doing. *"God is not a man, that he should lie"* (**Numbers 23:19**). Because *"God cannot lie"* (**Titus 1:2**), He will never offer something to someone that He doesn't intend to give! *"Whosoever will"* means, whosoever will! God's *sovereignty* is always in perfect harmony with His *righteousness*!

- God is omniscient, and He 'predestines' steps and pathways for those believing individuals whose exercise of *free-will* He foresees and *foreknows.*

- The third empowering (*soul*) Baptism with the Holy Spirit (*not salvation*) is the gift that's **limited** to those who have already been redeemed.

Properly understanding the origin of man's faith and the distinction of the three baptisms, helps unravel the first four of the Calvinistic "TULIP" difficulties of Reformed theology. Understanding the subsequent-to-salvation 'baptism *with* the Holy Spirit' further clarifies the Calvinists' misplaced "election" and "limited atonement" points.

2. Eternal Security vs. Falling from Grace

Similarly, the remedy to heal the arguments for and against the doctrine of "eternal security" again hinge on a clarified Biblical understanding of 'baptisms.' The born-again believer is baptized by the Spirit of God unto salvation, in that his human spirit has been quickened from death unto (eternal) life. God is, among other divine attributes; omniscient, omnipotent, and immutable. God knows the end from the beginning, is never surprised, and doesn't change his mind because of 'unforeseen' circumstances that He may have previously been impervious to. Therefore, if God sovereignly gives this (eternal) life, it is permanent. No one who receives it by faith can lose it or have it taken away (**Ephesians 2:1-10; Colossians 2:13-14; 1 Peter 3:18; John 10:28-29**). However, there is much warning in the Scriptures against 'falling away' and forfeiting available blessings:

- The Holy Spirit's quickening of our human spirits in the work of salvation is irreversible and *eternal*. His calling and giftings are also without repentance.

- The Holy Spirit's divine enablement and His empowering anointing can be *withdrawn* from the disobedient servant for a season, or even for the remainder of his lifetime if the disobedience is persistent and unrepented of.

- Again, the genuine believer's salvation is never in jeopardy, and God's gifts and calling are without repentance. But, deliberate and persistent disobedience affects man's sanctification and his effectiveness for service. This backsliding occurs in the soul of man, and can even result in disqualification from service (ministry) and loss of rewards, but not perdition.

3. Cessationism vs. Continuationism

The "Cessationist" (*one who believes the manifestational gifts of the Spirit have ceased*), armed with a few isolated and noncontextual Bible passages, insists on believing that the Holy Spirit has ceased His manifestational, so-called '*sign giftings*' to the post-1st Century Church. The Cessationist, however, may be helped by a fresh look at the Church's mission and the significance of the 'baptism' distinctions. The determined Cessationist, often with distrust and disdain for the "Continuationist" (*one who believes the Holy Spirit's giftings were intended to benefit the entirety of the Church Age, not just its first century*), will resist or re-interpret Scriptural evidence that contradicts his view because not doing so will devastate much of his denominational doctrinal tradition.

As previously noted, some will go as far as reinterpreting or outright invalidating the first two (*apostles and prophets*) of the five-fold ministries given to the Church (**Ephesians 4:11**). Incredulously, Cessationists create support for this view from **Ephesians 2:20-21** by completely ignoring the immediate context and broader application! They claim the "*apostles and prophets*" cited in this passage were only needed for the foundation of the Church, not its building up over the Church Age. But contextually, that passage has all to do with the 'mystery' of gentiles and Jews, as fellow-citizens, ultimately sharing the same inheritance! The 'apostles' (New Testament) and 'prophets' (Old Testament) are a united foundation to a building completed together with Christ as its Cornerstone! (**Revelation 18:20, 21:12-14**)

Not realizing it, are Cessationists projecting what they accuse Continuationists of, by perhaps even themselves nearing the peril of violating God's final Biblical warning of **Revelation 22:18-19** (the stern warning of not *adding* to or *taking away* from His Word)? In light of the Kingdom of God, Cessationists need to consider these truths:

4-Fold progressive Mission of the New Testament Church, in order:

- The *first* mission of the Church is to *worship God*;
- The *second* mission is to *edify*, *disciple*, and *minister to believers*;
- The *third* is to *evangelize the lost of the world*;
- The *fourth* is to be 'salt and light' in the earth, (**Matthew 5:13-16**).

This 4-Fold Mission is progressive, and listed in order of priority. As the Shorter Westminster Catechism of 1647 correctly states in its answer to the very first question; "*The chief end of man is to glorify God, and to enjoy Him for ever;* **1 Corinthians 10:31**." Achieving worship that is in 'spirit and truth' can then render the Church in the proper spiritual condition to successfully disciple believers. The God-given spiritual giftings to the Church are more about the internal building up and maturing of believers, than for external recruitment! Gifted and discipled believers can then thereafter effectively evangelize the world. The overall result is the Church's Godly influence of 'salt and light' in the world for Christ, that God intended for the Church to be a witness of.

The Three Christian Baptisms:

- Salvation is the Spirit's 'quickening' of the *human spirit* (*1st*), to then be publicly declared by the born-again believer through obedience unto water baptism (*2nd*);

- The subsequent baptism with the Holy Spirit (*3rd*, of the *soul*) is not for salvation, but for the *believer's aid* as are all of the spiritual giftings, benefitting both the individual and the corporate Body of believers;

- All of God's giftings can be properly used, unused, or abused – nevertheless, they were clearly provided for *perfecting* the saints and *edifying* the Church.

The three categories of spiritual gifts, with their sub-types,

(*prioritized in* **1 Corinthians 12:28**, *as explained in Ch. 9, sect. C-3 of this book*):

- <u>Ministry</u> gifts – the five listed in **Ephesians 4:11**

- <u>Motivational</u> gifts – the seven listed in **Romans 12:6-8** (+ one in **1 Peter 4:9-10**)

- <u>Manifestational</u> gifts – the nine listed in **1 Corinthians 12:7-10**

Permanency of the Five-fold Ministry of the Church:

- *Apostleship* – Some may omit apostleship as a viable continuing *office*, nevertheless the *gift* of apostleship was surely intended for the entire Church Age.

- *Prophets* – Some completely dilute, by redefining the prophetic to mean any proclaimer of God's Word [i.e., *'forth-telling'*], denying any possibility for *fore-telling*, or the true prophetic significance of the 'word of knowledge' (revelation of something *past* or *present* – i.e., **Acts 5:3**) and 'word of wisdom' (revelation of something or instruction of something for the *future* – i.e., **Acts 21:11**) gifts.

- *Evangelists* – Not commonly misinterpreted.

- *Pastors* – Not commonly misinterpreted, but some insist on the application of the 'Granville-Sharp Rule' for the Greek translation of **Ephesians 4:11** that effectively combines the Pastor-Teacher office as a singular gift.

- *Teachers* – Not commonly misinterpreted. It's acknowledged that there are teachers who do not also hold the office of pastor.

The born-again believer is admonished to keep on being filled with the Holy Spirit (**Ephesians 5:18**), because our still-sinful souls 'leak' and require continual replenishment. Our salvation is secure, but our anointing and empowerment for service can wane. Yet we don't despair! Because God's promise to us is that His gifts and calling are without repentance (**Romans 11:29**), we can come to Him continually for renewal and revival! Some of the believers present on the day of Pentecost when the Holy Spirit's empowerment was first dispensed (**Acts 2:4**), were also present when a re-filling came (**Acts 4:31**). But if we neglect this duty of replenishment, or persist in sinfulness, or if we fail to properly respond to God's corrective discipline, though we won't forfeit our salvation, we certainly can lose our unction, position, and effectiveness of service to Him (**Judges 16:20,28; Psalms 51:10-12; 1 Timothy 1:18-20; 1 Corinthians 9:27**). Stubborn disobedience may even cost us our earthly lives and certainly God's rewards, yet all without endangering our eternal salvation which is secure in Christ (**1 Corinthians 3:15, 5:5**).

B. The Soul Solution of Faith

1. The Battlefield of the Soul

We've concluded that sinful man's dead spirit was made alive when it was regenerated by the Holy Spirit at conversion to Christ. This creates in man the ability and an inner desire to commune with God while living out his life on the earth. However, the pre-glorified body of man remains in its carnal state after regeneration and is subject to many of the same sinful inclinations and passions that challenged him before salvation. Man is now awakened to the wrongfulness of those sinful passions, and he may well train himself to steer away from them, but this vulnerability never ceases to exist during his pre-glorified earthly lifetime. This spiritual struggle occurs in the mind, the emotions, and the will of man; i.e., his *soul*.

Man is especially tested either when all is well and he becomes complacent by letting his spiritual guard down, or when he despairs over things going wrong in life. The lowering of one's guard when all is well can occur when man begins to feel self-sufficient and unwittingly develops a dulled sense for his need of God. Satan can use this opening to begin tempting him beyond his own imagined ability to resist. Another scenario is when life does not go as smoothly as the expectations that one sets up for himself, thereby allowing Satan another open door through which he can bring disappointment, discouragement, anger, bitterness, unbelief, despair, and temptation.

The balanced Christian life is one of trusting-faith in the absolute faithfulness of God to complete the work He started, unto glorification (**Philippians 1:6**). The work started is regeneration. The completion God desires for us requires the inclusion of our obedience with discipline of the mind, control of the emotions, and determination of the will. God's quickening of our spirits creates a new awareness of His great goodness, as well as a deep desire to serve and please God. This newness can be euphoric and is perhaps more often recognized immediately after being born again, especially if it was a dramatic conversion with deliverance from a recognizably dominant destructive sin. But to all, the victorious Christian walk in this corrupt world will soon prove itself a challenging endeavor. The Comforter was sent to assist regenerated man's soul as an aid to overcoming these life's difficulties. All of us, Reformed, Baptists, Pentecostals, have had similar experiences, face the same challenges, and have at our disposal the same giftings and weapons of spiritual warfare.

2. The Comforter of the Soul

How does the Holy Spirit comfort the soul? First, we concluded that the Comforter, the very same Holy Spirit that regenerates the human spirit at salvation, is available to 'come upon' and fill man's soul for illumination and empowerment. Jesus said of the Comforter, "*...for he dwelleth with you, and shall be in you. I will not leave you comfortless: I will come to you*," (**John 14:17b-18**). Observe the contrast of a peoples who are void of a soul-comforter; "*For these things I weep; mine eye, mine eye runneth down with water, because the comforter that should relieve my soul is far from me: my children are desolate, because the enemy prevailed*," (**Lamentations 1:16**).

Secondly, He is the Spirit of Truth. The Word of God is powerful and able to provide the spiritual nourishment that man needs to feed his soul. Jesus said, "*...the Comforter, which is the Holy Ghost, whom the Father will send in my name, he shall teach you all things, and bring all things to your remembrance, whatsoever I have said unto you*," (**John 14:26**). Jesus added, "*...when the Comforter is come, whom I will send unto you from the Father, even the Spirit of truth, which proceedeth from the Father, he shall testify of me*,' (**John 15:26**). At the appropriate times of need, the Holy Spirit will help us to remember that which we have heard of God's Word. He will comfort and remind us of Jesus, his teaching, his promises, and His accomplished work on our behalf.

Finally, the Comforter will reveal to us things to come. Jesus said, "*...when he, the Spirit of truth, is come, he will guide you into all truth: for he shall not speak of himself; but whatsoever he shall hear, that shall he speak: and he will show you things to come. He shall glorify me: for he shall receive of mine, and shall show it unto you*" (**John 16:13-14**). This was accomplished through the New Testament writers, especially seen where revealed eschatological truth was recorded. However, Jesus also told us that when severe persecution comes, "*...when they shall lead you, and deliver you up, take no thought beforehand what ye shall speak, neither do ye premeditate: but whatsoever shall be given you in that hour, that speak ye: for it is not ye that speak, but the Holy Ghost*" (**Mark 13:11**). The '*word of knowledge*' and '*word of wisdom*' gifts will be in operation!

Therefore, we've concluded that the saved individual's spirit is regenerated from death unto life by the Spirit of God. This 'quickening' is a gift of God which is secure and eternal. The Scriptures insist that, "*...the gifts and calling of God are without repentance*" (**Romans 11:29**). Since the spirit of man is in a constant state, either dead or alive, unable without God's intervention to transition from spiritual "death' to spiritual 'life,' and since the body of man remains unchanged until glorification, the facts again lead us to the conclusion that the soul of man is where spiritual battles take place. It is the soul (*intellect, emotions, and will*) that is in dire need of the Comforter's help.

Again, all of us believers, Reformed, Baptist, and Pentecostal, need the Helper's comfort. He gives us illumination, recall, discernment, empowerment, and revelation.

3. The Empowerment of the Soul

The challenge to regenerated man's soul is not merely the mundane hardships of life, such as the ability to make a good living, illnesses, material lackings, victimization by others' abuses, etc. It is a spiritual warfare that we're engaged in! We are warned that, "*...we wrestle not against flesh and blood, but against principalities, against powers, against the rulers of the darkness of this world, against spiritual wickedness in high places*" (**Ephesians 6:12**). Satan is lurking about, "*seeking whom he may devour*" (**1 Peter 5:8b**). We are therefore counseled to, "*...resist (him) stedfast in the faith*" (**1 Peter 5:9a**). Happily, we are not left to accomplish this by our own strength or determination. Jesus told us that, "*...ye shall receive power, after that the Holy Ghost is come upon you*" (**Acts 1:8a**). We are exhorted to, "*...be strong in the Lord, and in the power of his might*" (**Ephesians 6:10**). We accomplish this by putting on, "*...the whole armour of God*" (**Ephesians 6:11a**), and by, "*Praying always with all prayer and supplication in the Spirit*" (**Ephesians 6:18a**).

Besides the Holy Spirit's comforting aid to all believers, and the heightened intimacy experience received from the baptism with the Holy Spirit severally given to believers who will receive it, there are also the *motivational, ministry*, and the varied *manifestational* gifts of the Spirit for the conventional and supernatural aid of the whole Church and its mission! God's gateway of entry is through the spirit of man. But the fruit and manifestation of His presence and power flow outward through the soul of man. We need all that God has to offer to us, especially in these last days. I say it again, if the early Church needed God's supernatural anointing to endure persecution, how much more will the end-time Church need the same, and that more abundantly!

The conclusion from the **Ephesians 6** chapter is that we must reinforce our souls with truth and righteousness (in the *mind*), by purposefully following the gospel (with our *wills*), and by faith in the assurance of salvation and the Word of God (in our *emotions*). This is the "*armour*" that we are instructed to put on. But God also gives us a power that we cannot put on through the studiously observant, obedient, and disciplined Christian life. The baptism with the Holy Spirit and His continual infilling, empowers and enables us for service, and the Spirit also helps us to pray effectively. The Apostle Paul said, "*Likewise the Spirit helpeth our infirmities: for we know not what we should pray for as we ought: but the Spirit itself maketh intercession for us with groanings which cannot be uttered. And he that searcheth the hearts knoweth what is the mind of the Spirit, because he maketh intercession for the saints according to the will of God*" (**Romans 8:26-27**).

These benefits from the Holy Spirit are for all believers. But those who trust Christ sufficiently to believe not only for salvation, but also the Father's giftings that were made available through Christ, will experience an added measure of anointing that empowers!

We have concluded that the baptism *with* the Holy Spirit is God's gift of the Spirit's power to enable us to receive illumination, serve, and overcome with an ability that enhances the necessary conventional means of prayer, Bible study, corporate worship and fellowship. This baptism is in no way an alternative to, and it does not take the place of conventional means. It does not render conventional means optional, nor does it devalue or minimize the importance and essentiality of those conventional means. It is simply an added benefit that God provides for his redeemed children who will by faith receive it. The baptism with the Holy Spirit without the conventional disciplines leads to arrogance, spiritual ignorance, and doctrinal errors. We are to prayerfully test every experience by the superior and eternal Word of God. As has been stated repeatedly, this 'baptism' is not the Holy Spirit's 'regenerational' baptism of man's spirit unto salvation, which can occur only once. It is a subsequent infusion of power by God's Spirit into the soul of man, which, because of its inclination for weakening and backsliding, needs constant discipline, as well as reviving, filling, and refilling.

Finally, we determined from the time-line we examined, that the promise of the Father was received by Jesus for dispensation to us after his ascension and glorification at the right hand of the Father. Therefore, it was separate and subsequent to the breathing of the regenerating Holy Spirit into the disciples by the resurrected, pre-ascended Christ. Allow me to try and explain it this way as well: Since the start of His earthly ministry, Jesus had already been authorized to bestow eternal life to as many as the Father would draw to His Son (**John 17:2**). Jesus did just that for the believing disciples on the evening of Resurrection Day, immediately after the atonement process had been eternally concluded by His resurrection. This is when Jesus breathed on them to receive the regenerational Holy Spirit baptism (**John 20:22**). But it took another fifty days before the empowering baptism was dispensed on the Day of Pentecost. Jesus explained it was essential for Him to ascend into heaven to personally receive this gift from the Father in order to then pour it out on his Church by the Holy Spirit (**John 14:16-18**; **16:7**; **Acts 2:33**). The authority to grant eternal life to believers drawn by the Father, and to raise them on the last day (**John 6:44**), had already been established. But the Spirit empowering gift is subsequent, and required Jesus to ascend in order to receive it and dispense it to the Church.

The validity of this subsequent promise did not cease at the conclusion of the first Century. Instead, as the Apostle Peter proclaimed on the day of Pentecost, we can expect the New Testament church to experience the baptism with the Holy Spirit until the Second Coming of Christ. Peter was specific when he said, "*For the promise is unto you, and to your children, and to all that are afar off, even as many as the Lord our God shall call*" (**Acts 2:39**). Again, this "Promise," was not regeneration, but rather, empowerment!

C. Unity of the Faith

In summary, a unifying understanding of the diverse doctrinal positions can be reconciled as follows:

T.U.L.I.P.

- **Total Depravity** – Yes, but to "*every man*" is given "*the measure of faith*," sufficient to receive God's grace if his faith is willfully exercised **(Romans 12:3)**.

- **Unconditional Election** – Yes, this is how the manifestational gifts are sovereignly dispensed. Yet they must be received by faith **(Mark 6:5-6; 9:24)**.

- **Limited Atonement** – Yes, the baptism *with* the Holy Spirit and manifestational gifts are reserved only for the already saved. Jesus explained it this way in his analogy, *"Neither do men put new wine* (Holy Spirit empowerment) *into old bottles* (unregenerated men), **(Matthew 9:17)**.

- **Irresistible grace** – We've seen how God's grace is powerful enough to surmount all iniquity, and yet it can be ignored, resisted, and even rejected.

- **Preservation of the Saints** – Yes, God foreknows and can't un-foresee his called!

2) Security -vs- Falling

- **Security** – Yes, our salvation is secure, and our giftings are without repentance.

- **Falling** – Yes, we can fall from God-given opportunities or positions of service, but not from His saving grace.

3) Cessation -or- Continuation of the Giftings

- **Continuation** – Yes, God ministers to us through the gifts of the Spirit for the duration of the '*third season*' (*referred to on pg. 115*) – i.e., the Church Age.

- **Cessation** – Yes, at the 'Parousia' and thereafter – from the time of Christ's Second Coming, we will ever be with Him and will no longer need the temporally given gifting aids.

When we view all these issues from the three-dimensional perspective offered in this book (the investigative prism of "*divine triangulation*" - as also seen in the differing baptisms), the controversies over sovereignty, eternal security, and spiritual gifts diminish. The contentions between fellow believers over free-will, the possibility of losing one's salvation, the baptism with the Holy Spirit and giftings are eased. The three-dimensional understanding provides the key to unlock the bridge over these unnecessary doctrinal chasms, thus linking closer together all the dear brethren of like-precious faith.

Are not all fellow-believers in Christ Jesus those who share the common desire and commitment to *"walk not after the flesh, but after the Spirit"* (**Romans 8:1**)? If so, we are not under condemnation and share our places on God's winning team. We need each other! This is so, especially as Christ's Second Coming events draw nearer. The Church so very much needs the sober intellectual contributions of the Reformed believers, the faithful soul-winning disciplines of the Baptist believers, and also the anointed discernment and enablement of the 'Spirit-filled' believers.

We are in the Church Age, the *'third season of the Spirit,'* (**Hebrews 1:1-2; John 16:7**). In each Season God revealed a new Person of the Godhead without replacing or diminishing the former. The Spirit is manifestly at work in our day. Some denying cessationists who "hear" from God are actually operating in some form of the manifestational gifts without even realizing it! We must all be filled with the Spirit, grounded in His Word and actively operating in His giftings!

Allow me a final exhortation: The Apostle Paul wrote, *"Behold therefore the goodness and severity of God: on them which fell, severity; but towards thee, goodness, if thou continue in his goodness: otherwise thou shalt also be cut off,"* (**Romans 11:22**). As a basis for this verse, we must consider God's "Righteousness." A good definition for God's *righteousness* is *not* that God is 'always right,' (*although that's not untrue*). God's 'righteousness' is all of His divine attributes (or *'eternal perfections'*) in perfect harmony with one another. With God, what to us is incompatible, is righteousness with Him! God is uncompromisingly holy, and yet continually and faithfully merciful (**Lamentations 3:22-23**). Likewise, God is perfectly just, but also longsuffering. He is unwaveringly just, yet generously forgiving. It is the goodness (*not judgment*) of God that leads us to repentance (**Romans 2:4**), yet His severity leads to judgment. God's "mercy" is not giving us the judgment we deserve, while God's "grace" is giving us the blessings we don't deserve! This is all because of Jesus' victorious atoning work on the Cross!

What I believe Paul is teaching the Church in **Romans 11:22** (*beyond the immediate discussion of the Jews' destiny*), is that we all stand in a 'neutral' place between His blessings and judgment. Yes, those who are outside of Christ are *"condemned already"* (**John 3:18**), but before the final declaration of condemnation we all have equal opportunity to either receive salvation in Christ, or to remain on an inevitable destiny of judgment outside of Christ. Those who enter in to salvation through Christ are eternally secure. But those who unrepentantly and rebelliously resist Christ, and find pleasure in doing so, God may give *"over to a reprobate mind"* (**Romans 1:28-32**), bringing them ever closer to certain judgment.

Through Abraham's successful negotiations, God's goodness and mercy was extraordinary to the undeserving Sodomites (**Genesis 18-19**), being willing to spare them if only 10 (*out of an estimated population in Sodom, Gomorrah & Zoar of 150,000*) would repent. That means, just .00667% of the 150,000 could have spared the nation! Yet, why I fear for America is that *"judgment must begin at the house of God"* (**1 Peter 4:17**). Does America, the only nation in the history of the world to be founded on Judeo-Christian principles, have within it a mere 23,310 aware, believing and repentant intercessors (*.00667% of the United States' current population of 350,000 million*)? Are there a mere 466 alert believers in each of the 50 States? Even in New York State, NYC being the 'portal' of the return of wickedness in America (as described by Jonathan Cahn in his *The Return of the Gods* book), if every one of the 62 NY Counties had but a miniscule Spirit-filled 7.5 intercessors each, judgment might well be stayed!

On the 'severity' side, the prophet Ezekiel repeatedly declared (**Ezekiel 14:13-22**), that when judgment has been determined upon an unrepentant nation, even if three of the greatest intercessors (**2 Peter 2:5**; **Daniel 6:10**; **Job 1:4-5**), *"Noah, Daniel, and Job were in it,"* the three of them alone would be delivered, but all the rest, including their sons and daughters, would not escape the end-time type of judgment calamities described as His *"four sore judgments...the sword, and the famine, and the noisome beast, and the pestilence"* (the *"beginning of* *sorrows*" – **Matthew 24:4-8**). But God's goodness yet prevails (**Ezek. 14:22**) in that a "*remnant*"…would be brought forth (**Matthew 24:29-31** - 'rapture') of "*both sons and daughters*"! …Behold therefore, *both* the goodness and severity of God!

This is not the time to continue nurturing divisions within the Body of Christ. Those who believe God and His Word are now being more and more regarded as 'extremist haters.' Those who reject God, His promises, and even the nature of His creation, are deemed to be the 'free' and 'enlightened.' But we (*believers*) are called "*watchmen*" (**Ezekiel 3:17**), commissioned to both "*hear*" and "*give warning.*"

As stated, we (the Reformed, Baptists & "Charismatics") all need each other, especially so in these last days! Hypothetically, what if we could join forces and borrow from each other's strengths in our evangelistic efforts, by utilizing the Baptists to prayerfully organize the campaign, the Pentecostals to lead the worship and prayers, and the Reformed to articulate the Word? Perhaps as things are, it might only be a distant dream. But if we could come to a more unified Biblical understanding and anointing, sharing the same goals, it just might be a glorious honor to our Savior! After all, we'll all be together as one in heaven! (**Matthew 6:10**; **Luke 11:2**)

May God use "SOUL BAPTISM," to work towards the unity of His Church, the accomplishment of His perfect purposes for His glory, and for the soon complete disclosure of His coming Kingdom. Amen.

SCRIPTURE REFERENCE INDEX

(Bold text references with their page numbers refer to Scripture verses used for the Chapter headings, as indicated within the parenthesis)

Revelation (cont.)

Bibliography

Abel, George O. *Realm of the Universe.* Philadelphia: Saunders College, 1980.

Archer, Gleason L. *Encyclopedia of Bible Difficulties.* Grand Rapids: Zondervan, 1982.

Armerding, Carl E., W. Ward Gasque, ed. *A Guide to Biblical Prophecy.* Peabody, MA: Hendrickson Publishers, 1989.

Barton, Austin. *Trichotomy: A Study of the Spirit, Soul & Body.* Tulsa: Harrison House, 1976.

Boa, Kenneth. *GOD, I Don't Understand.* Wheaton: Victor Books, 1976.

Boa, Kenneth, et. al., (Contributors to Study Aids). *The Open Bible – Expanded Edition.* Nashville: Nelson, 1985.

Brandt, Robert L., Zenas J. Bicket. *The Spirit Helps Us Pray: A Biblical Theology of Prayer.* Springfield, MO: Logion Press, 1997.

Buswell, J. Oliver. *A Systematic Theology of the Christian Religion.* Grand Rapids: Zondervan, 1976.

Cahn, Jonathan. *The Return of the Gods.* Lake Mary, FL: FrontLine/Charisma Media, 2022.

Camping, Harold. *1994?.* New York: Vantage Press, 1992.

Douglas, J.D., Philip W. Comfort, eds. *Who's Who in Christian History.* Wheaton: Tyndale House, 1992.

Durant, Will. *The Story of Civilization: Part II.* New York: Simon & Schuster, 1939.

Enns, Paul. *The Moody Handbook of Theology.* Chicago: Moody Press, 1989.

Ervin, Howard M. *Spirit Baptism.* Peabody, MA: Hendrickson Publishers, 1987.

Flynn, Leslie B. *19 Gifts of the Spirit.* Wheaton: Victor Books, 1994.

Goodall, Wayde. *Why Great Men Fall.* Green Forest, AR: New Leaf Press, 2005.

Guthrie, Donald. *New Testament Theology.* Downers Grove, IL: Inter-Varsity Press, 1981.

Hanegraaff, Hank. *Counterfeit Revival.* Dallas: Word Publishing, 1997.

Henry, Matthew. *Matthew Henry Commentary on the Holy Bible, Vol. 3.* Nashville: Royal Publishers, 1979.

Hordern, William E. *A Layman's Guide to Protestant Theology.* New York: Macmillan Publishing, 1968.

Inglis, Stuart J. *Physics: An Ebb and Flow of Ideas.* New York: John Wiley & Sons, 1970.

Lewis, CS. *Mere Christianity.* San Francisco: Harper Collins Publishers, 1952. Lockyer, Herbert. *All the Doctrines of the Bible.* Grand Rapids: Zondervan, 1964.

MacArthur, John F. Jr. *Charismatic Chaos.* Grand Rapids: Zondervan, 1992.

McQuaid, Elwood. *The Outpouring.* Bellmawr, NJ: The Friends of Israel Gospel Ministry, 1990.

Morris, Henry M. *The Bible and Modern Science.* Chicago: Moody Press, 1951.

Nee, Watchman. *The Latent Power of the Soul.* New York: Christian Fellowship Publishers, 1972.

_____*he Normal Christian Life.* Wheaton, IL: Tyndale House, 1983.

Rosenthal, Marvin. *The Pre-Wrath Rapture of the Church.* Nashville: Thomas Nelson Publishers, 1990.

Rosenthal, Stan. *One God or Three?*. Orlando: Zion's Hope, 1997.

Ruiz, Luis C. *The Battle for Biblical Baptism*. Cleveland, GA: The Old Paths Publications, 2020.

Scheffel, Richard L. ed. *ABC's of Nature*. Pleasantville, NY: Reader's Digest Assoc., 1984.

Showers, Renald. *Angels*. Bellmawr, NJ: Friends of Israel, 1997.

Sproul, R.C. *The Holiness of God*. Wheaton: Tyndale House, 1985.

_____*The Mystery of the Holy Spirit*. Wheaton: Tyndale House, 1990.

Stone, Nathan. *Names of God*. Chicago: Moody Press, 1944.

Strom, Andrew. *Great Healing Revivalists: How God's Power Came*. (c.1996). www.christianword.org/revival/healing.html

Strong, James. *Strong's Greek Dictionary of the New Testament*. Nashville: Crusade Bible Publishers.

Sumrall, Lester. *Spirit, Soul and Body*. New Kensington: Whitaker House, 1995.

Swaggart, Jimmy. *Gifts of the Spirit*. Baton Rouge, LA: Jimmy Swaggart Ministries, 1985.

_____*Questions & Answers*. Baton Rouge, LA: Jimmy Swaggart Ministries, 1985.

Thiessen, Henry Clarence. *Lectures in Systematic Theology*. Grand Rapids: Eerdman's Publishing Co., rev. ed. 1979.

Unger, Merrill. *Demons in the World Today*. Wheaton: Tyndale House, 1971.

Wilkerson, David. *Set the Trumpet to Thy Mouth*. Lindale, TX: World Challenge, 1985.

www.ingramcontent.com/pod-product-compliance
Lightning Source LLC
Chambersburg PA
CBHW051522120626
46551CB00012B/1042